MAIN STREET
WAS
TWO BLOCKS
LONG

MAIN STREET
WAS
TWO BLOCKS
LONG

Norene Murphey Hokett

RUTLEDGE HILL PRESS
Nashville, Tennessee

Copyright © Norene Murphey Hokett

Published in Nashville, Tennessee, by Rutledge Hill Press, 211 Seventh Avenue, North, Nashville, Tennessee 37219

Typography by D&T/Bailey, Inc., Nashville, Tennessee

Library of Congress Cataloging-in-Publication Data

Hokett, Norene Murphey, 1932–
    Main street was two blocks long / Norene Murphey Hokett.
      p. cm.
    ISBN 1-55853-263-3 : $16.95
    1. City and town life—Middle West—Fiction. 2. Family—
Middle West—Fiction. I. Title.
    PS3558.0347736M35 1993
    813′.54—dc20
                                   93-29407
                                       CIP

Printed in the United States of America
1 2 3 4 5 6 — 97 96 95 94 93

IN MEMORY OF
DADDY AND MOTHER

CONTENTS

FOREWORD

Life in small town America in the forties and fifties thrived on everyday events—the rise and the fall of the little things, the trivia of what people said and did. The joys and sorrows of never-to-be-famous blended with national and international events to weave a fabric of existence that was to become known as Americana.

From weather to war the rhythm and heartbeat of our little town could have been any community from sixty to sixty thousand. We knew each other, and we cared. We were not just numbers on a census taker's report or a nondescript family on the block.

Our families and neighbors were labeled good or bad. For the most part, morals were measured at the churches, ingrained in the schools, and lived out in the streets. Despite local rumors to the contrary, there was an overall optimism that things ultimately would turn out all right in the end because, after all, this was America.

My vantage point on Main Street was from the front window of my parents' restaurant, Jeff's Café. Much more than food crossed over its counters. The townsfolk and those of neighboring communities came to eat and talk over life's latest momentous events. Life and death, and everything in between, were dramatized on the most neutral stage of all, the town's dining table. It was there I watched, innocently, the unfolding drama of life on Main Street.

9

INTRODUCTION

"THIS IS YOUR OLD FRIEND, CAROLYN," the voice on my telephone receiver announced. "This year we are celebrating our forty-second high school class reunion. It won't be complete without you. Let's get together and relive our good times again. Remember when . . ." and our minds reconnected from half a lifetime ago as we again walked those once familiar sidewalks—giggling and young with adventure and excitement.

Carolyn's voice had not changed, yet her southwestern accent had been softened with thirty-nine years of living on Central Park West in New York City. By comparison, I answered her questions and reminisced with the added vocal values of southern California glossed across my drawl.

The years fell away—we were girls again on Main Street in a small Oklahoma town. Her dad owned the only chicken hatchery, and mine owned one of the many cafés.

My town was like many found in small communities across America at the end of the 1930s. There was the corner drugstore and the one and only movie theater—there had been two for a while, but only one survived. There were a couple of grocery stores, the Farmer's National Bank, two dry goods stores, and the TG&Y five-and-ten-cent store. It was possible then to buy a few items for a nickel and a dime.

11

First Baptist Church was on Main Street, but it was the biggest church in town so that was only fair. First Methodist and First Christian were on side streets but still considered "downtown," and a Pentecostal church and a Church of Christ were near the edge of town. There also was a Catholic Church, but it was only open one Sunday a month and everybody knew it was necessary to go to church more than that to be a Christian.

An ice plant occupied one end of those two blocks, and a chiropractic clinic was across from the Baptist Church at the other end. In addition, there was a grain elevator, which stayed busy with trucks coming and going during wheat harvest in the summer.

Our little town didn't straddle the highway that connected it to the rest of civilization. We were off center of it by two or three blocks. Tourists lost from the main highway had to make an effort to come downtown. They occasionally did, to buy gas or get a good plate of fried chicken and hot yeast rolls. Those once-lost tourists and truck drivers got lost on a regular basis so they could eat at my parents' restaurant, Jeff's Café.

The only high school and junior high was off the highway a half block or so, while the first four grades were housed in a tall, fierce-looking old building on the other side of the small artery. The townsfolk had constructed an underpass under the highway so little kids would be protected from traffic. As a child, I would have preferred traffic to that dreaded dark underpass.

There was a small hospital in town just across from the post office, volunteer fire department, and one-cell city jail. Tonsils were removed at the hospital and so were appendixes, but sick folk were transferred to Oklahoma City for more serious, long-term care.

We had a funeral home that did a regular business because it was the only one around. The Goodyear store sold tires and new bicycles and had a great selection of toys at Christmas, while the local tire shop fixed old tires and sold the retreaded ones.

The bakery seemed to do most of its business early in the morning from the smell of the freshly baked bread. There was a blacksmith's shop that clanged and banged a succession of horseshoes onto almost every saddlehorse in the community, and there were enough horse owners to keep a saddle shop in business. It sold hand-tooled boots and saddles, many of them made to match.

Two or three barbershops kept the men's hair trimmed for miles around while two or three beauty shops did a thriving business in permanent waves, weekly shampoos, and sets.

For excitement there was the local fairgrounds where the 4-H'ers showed their animals for the first time each year and where the yearly county fair was held in the first days of early fall. Blue ribbons were won for everything from prize pigs and cattle to handmade quilts and home-made pickles.

The rest of the year there was the movie theater showing Hollywood's best when it was at its peak as Tinseltown, U.S.A. Barbara Stanwyck and Clark Gable kept our attention during the week, and Roy Rogers and Gene Autry did a roaring business on weekends. For a diversion, a traveling roller rink hit town every few months, and the local young people would skate their hearts out under a big tent. On warm nights the sides could be rolled up and when the town closed down just before sundown, parking places were hard to find as young adults and old people alike parked all the way around the tent to watch the roller skaters do their best and occasionally their worst. When some good ole boy decided to learn to skate, he could get more attention than he could handle and stay upright.

Ours was a farming community—wheat, cotton, and soybeans. The farmers worked hard and kept at it for long hours.

During the week, Main Street was deserted. School was in session, but even it dismissed for up to two weeks for cotton picking. Because of that, school started the first week in August, at the height of Oklahoma's summer heat, and we had no refrigerated air conditioning. The bank was the only place with that luxury.

In those early days of the year school was in session by 8:30 A.M. and out just after noon. Regular school days began when cotton picking was over.

Weekdays were quiet and lazy in town except during wheat harvest. Some businesses closed in the early afternoon, and almost everybody up and down Main Street was gone by 6:00 or 6:30 P.M. That included the drugstores and the pharmacy. In case of a dire pharmaceutical need, the Bell Telephone operator could raise anyone in town within a few minutes.

There seldom was grumbling or griping because a neighbor's needs were important. The illness was town talk by morning if it was serious.

In spite of the lazy look of local shops, our community throbbed with life made possible by long hours of hard work. Only on the weekends did the farm families take time from their fields. Saturday was a big day. By three o'clock on any Saturday afternoon, parking places were at a premium along those two main blocks, and young people cruised bumper to bumper, up and down and back again. To see and be seen—with whom, where, and in what car—was a community mating ritual. Proposals were made and engagement rings presented in that procession. It was a time to be savored.

The chaos and confusion reached a fever peak by 11:45 P.M. and the beginning of the midnight movie. For two hours, sometimes more, the streets were hushed, the honking and hubbub stilled as movie magic held the community in a trance.

By 1:30 A.M. the silence was briefly broken when the movie ended. Horns honked, tires squealed, and the town settled down to another week of normal quiet activity.

Sunday was celebrated in respect. Briefly before 9:30 A.M., cars crawled into town. Their owners quietly parked them in front of the church of their choice. Families gathered and worshiped together while nonchurchgoers observed a day of rest. No businesses were open except for a tiny market out on the highway where the forgetful could purchase a loaf of bread or a pound of coffee. Families gathered for Sunday dinner, and the meal of the week was served by midafternoon. It was an occasion for visiting, a family-and-friends time. Sunday evening church was held at the main denominations, and those services were well attended. After-church socials, and in the summer ice cream suppers and watermelon feasts, added to the social life.

It was America's growing-up years before the last mighty migration began from the farm to the city—from children living across town to brothers and sisters living across the nation. America changed from crowded Main Streets to ten-lane freeways, from names to ZIP code numbers.

We left our hometowns to live in New York and California, and many of those little communities became ghost towns. We grew up, moved away, and lost touch. But most of us never forgot our hometowns.

We never forgot the stories, either, but we discovered each of us had formed a memory of our own in those years apart. And our memories didn't always match.

It was a time and place in history marked by family values. Moral virtues were considered important, and it was a time of "right and wrong." This was middle America in the forties and fifties.

The lives we lived are memories now, magnified by our imaginations. Stories change, are rearranged, and flow together with other incidents from other times. That is true of the stories found here. This isn't merely factual history. Names have been changed sometimes; incidents have become larger than life; and some of them may not have happened exactly as I remember them. But isn't that the way memories are?

MAIN STREET WAS TWO BLOCKS LONG

REUNION

As THE PLANE CIRCLED THE AIRPORT for landing, I glanced out the window. There had been a class reunion two years earlier, but I had decided to stand by my vow that I would "never go back again."

Now, two years later after many phone calls from former classmates, I had broken my vow. As I tugged my overfilled garment bag toward the rental car counter, I chided myself again. "Why am I doing this?" In spite of the wonder and magic of the phone calls, things wouldn't be the same. They couldn't. Forty-two years had passed. We would all be old and fat, gray or bald. Main Street would have changed, and so would the people on it. This was the nineties, and the things I had loved were memories. The reality of the present would shed a harsh light on the yesterdays I carried in my memory.

Over a hundred miles lay before me. As the rented Ford Escort gobbled up the miles, I smelled the sweet, clean smell of alfalfa hay and ripening grain. White-faced cattle grazed in green pastures, washed clean by the rain. Random drops still splashed the windshield as I rediscovered the red clay of Oklahoma visible along the roadside. The occasional houses were punctuated by a spired church or a grain elevator.

The turn off I-40 came sooner than I expected. A few minutes later, I was lost. A road sign had pointed between two narrow, poorly paved roads, directly into a cow pasture. I took the wrong road and found myself at a dead end. With a quick U-turn, I corrected the mistake and pushed hard on the gas pedal to make up for lost time. Five minutes later I was beside the road, pulled over by a highway patrolman! Eighty in a fifty-five miles per hour zone isn't recommended.

"But . . . but . . . I'm on my way to a reunion—a town reunion, really—of all the graduating classes in my hometown. I haven't been back in forty-two years, and I'm late—really late."

The patrolman was a southern gentleman. "Then ah might be ruinin' yo' fun if I gave ya' a ticket. Heah's a warnin' instead. But just rememba', honey, this ain't no California freeway!"

I looked at him with a sigh of relief. "I won't forget. And thanks!"

It was dark as I pulled up to "the barn" in the city park. Suddenly I was gripped with fear. No one would know me. I certainly didn't look the same. I was overweight from too much asthma medication and steroids due to recent asthmatic attacks. My hair was blonde now to cover the gray that had streaked the former brown. I was different, and they would be, too.

The beam of a flashlight cut through the darkness as two women passed the car. "Are you going to the reunion?" I asked. "I'd sure like to go with you."

"Love to have you," said the one with the flashlight. Then she beamed the light on my name tag.

"Norene! Remember me? I'm one of the Sullivan girls. I accompanied you in high school when you sang!"

"Yes, oh, yes. You were a terrific accompanist. How are you?"

The two were sisters, daughters of the town's doctor. They and their brothers had all gone into medicine.

As we walked into the reunion party, balloons and

streamers hung around the walls and from the ceiling. The crowd was mingling, talking, hugging, and giggling. Occasionally screeches of recognition were heard.

"She is here!" someone shouted. Suddenly I was surrounded by people and laughter. All of us stared at name tags. For some it was the only key to the past.

"Carolyn," I screamed. The tall, glamorous woman with a beautiful smile and I exchanged hugs.

"Donna!" Donna was the same, except with her iron-gray hair she reminded me of her mother.

Then there were Ray and Jack and Kenneth. Jack still had his impish smile and Ray his outgoing, friendly personality. Kenneth was ever the kind, soft-spoken one. Jack's dad had owned the newspaper, and he had been a newspaperman in San Jose, California, for thirty-five years.

Carolyn had been the class lover of the arts, the fashion plate. She had married, and now lived in New York City, where she is still involved in the arts. Along with her corporate lawyer husband, she had traveled the world. However, like mine, her heart remained entrenched in the warmth of family we had first discovered on Main Street.

Donna had been a fine student. She and her husband had built a successful investment company in the city. He had died suddenly of a heart attack three years previously. They had been childhood sweethearts, and as we talked there still seemed to be an empty place right at her shoulder where he always had stood.

As our circle tightened and our laughter increased, someone said, "Why don't we get in a corner, turn down the lights, and have Norene tell us another scary story. Do you ever tell stories anymore, Norene?"

"I surely do. Every day in class—and hey, you guys, I just wrote a book!"

"You didn't?"

"What about?"

"Oh it's a book of silly short stories about life on Main Street. I told about a lot of the crazy things we used to do and how fun it was to grow up here!"

"Great!"

"I even told about those oral book reports when I stretched mine into a week of chills and laughter in English class!"

"That wasn't silly, that was fun."

"Did you tell about the flood and the time . . ."

The laughter washed around us as we remembered our growing-up years. We stared into each other's faces, and the years fell away. We were young again. We recalled ball games, parties, romances, teachers, classes, and funny things had happened on Main Street. It and the times in which we lived had shaped the people we had become.

Yet, the ingredients of each of our personalities had signaled where we would go and what we would do. Jack had done what he had known when he went into the newspaper business. I was still telling stories in the classroom—I'd only changed states. Carolyn was still singing and involved in the arts—on a different and grander scale—while others had chosen to remain on Main Street.

Margerite was a housewife and our class representative. Jeanne had married and moved to another small town nearby to raise a family and take care of her husband and a comfortable home. Her parents, Elvina and Wade, lived one block away on the next street and were only two years away from their sixtieth wedding anniversary.

One or two people had broken their molds. Ray and his wife, Anita, lived in Delaware where he owned a fishing boat. He and his crew fished the Atlantic Ocean, while

Anita proudly announced to me that "she could filet a hundred fish in an hour!"

Most of our class was here. We were older, but not old. In a sense, we each had fulfilled our destinies. We had only been limited by our imaginations, creativity, and sense of self-worth.

Some had felt as I had, that they never wanted to come back. I hadn't wanted to destroy the memories. Who knows why others hadn't returned?

The buildings on Main Street were different—older or remodeled, but aged. The jail was still there—unused and abandoned. The post office and the First Methodist Church remained the same. The First Baptist Church had added on, but the sign out front was the same one that hung there when I was a child, an open Bible-shaped sign stating, "First Baptist Church, Preaching the Word." It had been lighted at night in neon as I grew up.

The funeral home had been remodeled, and the hospital sported a new wing. The fire station was still there, but the town had a real police car with lights on top! The Liberty Theater had been remodeled with an entirely new glass front.

Daddy's little café was a shambles. The downstairs was a junk shop or storage area, and a "closed" sign hung on the window, although the door was open. The rickety outside wooden stairway was gone, leaving a line on the brick where it had been. The upstairs two rooms appeared to have had a fire. The empty, dirty windows had a vacant stare, and one door hung crazily on its hinges. All signs of life were gone. It seemed to say, "No good could have ever happened here," but it had. Daddy's words rang again in my ears: "It isn't the buildings, it's the people inside that make the difference."

That is what the reunion was all about. People! Each in

our own way had lived out what we had started to live. We had become—and we were each still becoming— ourselves, and our lives are still rich with discovery.

As I drove back to the airport, my thoughts almost overpowered me as the landscape of childhood flashed past the window. A lifetime of memories had been relived in one weekend, and I had been filled with nostalgia.

The plane circled the airport as it ascended, and I stared down at the red Oklahoma clay. That place—that state—that town—Main Street and the values and morals I had learned there—had shaped me. I *had* come home again!

The more than 1,100 people who had returned to the reunion had moved on. But we were all still connected to each other by Main Street.

CARNEGIE, OKLAHOMA

DADDY

A BOOK WAS A TREASURE TO DADDY. Once he read a book, he never forgot it. In addition to his love for learning, he was the kindest man I have ever known. His face was aglow with pleasure because he was usually smiling. With his blue eyes twinkling and a faint smile on his face, he nearly always looked pleased. This man was my father.

Daddy seemed to influence almost everyone he met. That included me. He was an excellent speaker with a love for the use of beautiful language. Words were pictures, but they were more than that. The simple eloquence of a well-honed phrase thrilled him the most. This six-foot-tall man with a bald head twinkled when he talked.

Daddy loved humor. He'd laugh until the tears rolled at things said or jokes that were played on him. He loved people, and that love was returned a hundredfold. It always seemed to surprise him. He was a deep thinker and a deeply religious man, although his religious beliefs were lived, not discussed. That deep faith was not flaunted. He was one of the few truly humble people I have ever known.

Dad had a reverence for books. When I was little, we lived four or five miles from the nearest town. There was no television and no radio. We had no electricity, and neither did any of our neighbors. Electricity was for town people only. So after the chores were done, supper eaten, and the dishes washed and put away, mother would put a clean, freshly ironed tablecloth on the table and place the kerosene lamp in the middle. After Dad had washed and carefully dried his hands, he would get out the book we were reading together. We would gather around the table, and the story would continue.

My cousin Roy, who was seven years older than me, lived with us. Both of his parents had died, and Mother and Dad had made him another member of our family. As we sat around the table with the lamplight glowing, Daddy would keep us spellbound as he read one great book after another.

Because Daddy read dramatically so that we lived every scene, the pirates of *Treasure Island* stalked through our tiny kitchen loudly enough to raise goose pimples. More than once when Dad's chair accidently squeaked, I'd leap into Mother's lap for protection. I was certain it was the sound of the pirate dragging his wooden leg across the floor.

As the lamplight played across the faces around the table, the great masterpieces of literature were read to us as only Daddy could read them. We began the reading each night with the novel or the poetry we had been reading the previous night. Just before bedtime, with us still begging Daddy to continue, he would stop and quietly place the bookmark in the book to hold the place until the next night. Then he would bring out the old family Bible that was almost too large to use and read from it. As he turned the crisp old pages, often I would ask to see the family records. On those pages were recorded the births and deaths of Mother's family dating back to the early 1800s.

At school one day the teacher asked each one of us to share what we did in the evening. I proudly exclaimed that my Dad was reading us a guaranteed story. Everybody laughed but me.

"Do you mean if you don't like it, your dad will take it back?" she asked.

"No," I cried, "he just begins reading where he left off the night before."

"Then, you mean he reads a continued story," she informed me.

"No ma'am, it is guaranteed to start again the next night!"

From that time on, Daddy would look at me and smile knowingly as he announced, "We're having another guaranteed story."

Daddy enjoyed John Greenleaf Whittier's "Snowbound." It became one of our favorites, especially on snowy nights. When Daddy would get to the part about the cider simmering on the hearth, he would say, "Mother has stories too."

Mother would remember her childhood days in Ohio when the snow would blow and drift. "The fences would disappear completely, and a horse and sleigh were the only way people could travel from place to place." We were always eager to hear her recall stories of her girlhood days.

Then Mother would put cider on top of the cast-iron pot-bellied stove to simmer while Dad continued reading Whittier's poem. Then he'd stop, look around the table, and ask each of us to share our favorite story as we sipped cups of hot, cinnamony cider, which was one of the reasons we loved that poem so much.

Years later I was to stand in Whittier's home in Haverhill, Massachusetts, in the room with the big fireplace that had crackled so merrily. I ran my hand over the cracked mug that had held the cider described in his poem.

As I stood there savoring the place that had inspired the poem, I heard again, in my mind, Daddy's voice: "The sun that brief December day/Rose cheerless over hills of gray,/And, darkly circled, gave at noon/A sadder light than waning moon." Once more the lamplight flickered across those faces of my family, caught in the circle of the warm glow.

Two different families, two different states, separated in time by more than a century—but we were bound by a poem that vividly described what we had in common: the unbreakable cord of togetherness that only love can weave.

THE OLD SCHOOLHOUSE

THE OLD RED BRICK BUILDING SAT sternly astride the hill keeping grim vigil over the town below, the windows glaring with an unblinking stare. High atop the fourth floor was the belfry with a heavy cast-iron bell inside, the only decorative touch. The bell solemnly clanged out its message promptly at 8:30 each morning and again at 1:00 in the afternoon during the school year.

Moving to a new town and changing schools was a scary experience for me at the age of nine, but the sight of the unfriendly building on the hill filled me with additional apprehension. I had left a new school with light-filled classrooms and broad hallways with bulletin boards that displayed colorful samples of artwork created by the students. The contrasts in school settings alone were frightening. But Daddy had explained that people made the places, not the buildings themselves.

As I glanced up and down the dimly lighted hallways with their dark, heavy stairways dissecting overhead, I wasn't so sure. The boards in the floor groaned as if in pain under the weight of our feet. The air was stale, and the building smelled of years of chalk dust, old vegetable soup, and sweat-soaked gym socks. Each floor sported two naked low-voltage light bulbs at either end of the dim, spooky hallway. The middle rung of each stair was worn thin with a hollow place in the middle from the hundreds of feet that had climbed there over the years.

This building had been one of the first in town, and at one time, the entire school—kindergarten through twelfth grade—had been housed on these four floors. However, the population had grown, and a junior high and a high school had been built. Now only the first four grades attended here. I only had to survive these surroundings for one year.

Mounting the stairs, we discovered the principal's office was on the top floor. This old building, so out of step with the young minds it housed, had been built for a different generation. It was a generation that believed learning was bad medicine to be choked down without a smile and swallowed without laughter. Learning had been grim business back then.

However, the principal was in direct contrast to his rigid, crowded old office. He was a huge man who filled the doorway with his body and warm smile. Enrollment was accomplished quickly, and I found myself in the classroom next door with Daddy disappearing down the stairs.

Class started normally enough. I was assigned a desk, issued books, and introduced, but that orderly atmosphere was shattered with the ringing of the huge, cast-iron bell directly above our heads. The entire room vibrated with the sound that seemed to originate within our heads, so close was the bell.

"Fire! Everybody line up!" shouted the teacher.

It was then I noticed everyone facing the window instead of the door. A steel covering there had been removed, revealing a large, gapping black hole leading into darkness. The students were going to step into that hole. As the first students disappeared into the blackness in front of them, fear choked me.

"No, I can't do that. I'll go down the stairs," I screamed. But a deep masculine voice boomed behind me, "Step into the fire escape and sit down. You will be outside and downstairs in just a second. Do it *now.*"

The voice behind me was louder than my fear. Suddenly I had no other choice. Stepping into the hole, I found myself inside a huge, covered slide. This was the large, round steel tunnel I had seen attached to the building on the outside.

As I sat down and lifted my feet, cold air rushed up my dress and lifted my hair. It was a quick, cold ride that ended all too suddenly in shock. No one had told me to put my feet down when I reached the end of the tunnel, so I didn't. I shot through the opening at a greater speed than I'd ever traveled on a regular slide. I came to a sudden and terrible stop on the gravel covering the ground at the escape exit.

Gravel bit into my legs and bottom while cold air rushed into the fresh wounds. I screamed with pain and shock.

"Hey, new girl, why didn't you put your feet down?"

"Yeah, didn't anybody ever teach you to slide down a slide?"

"Look at her cry. What a baby!"

"Are you hurt, honey? I'm so sorry. Here, let me help you." The last voice was the big, masculine one that had ordered this chaos in the first place. But now the voice was warm, comforting, understanding.

The big hands that reached down to pick me up were gentle, tender hands that gradually began restoring my self-confidence. Mr. Lamb was a big man, but he must have been a father. He knew how to handle little kids who were scared, and I felt better already.

"You have had a full day, and it hasn't even started yet," he continued.

"My dress is dirty, my legs are bloody, and I just look awful." I cried as tears made furrows through the dirt on my face.

"You will be all right now," Mr. Lamb comforted. "I'll get you to the nurse's office where she will doctor those scrapes and clean you up. Then I'll call your dad and let him come and take you home. You have learned enough for one day."

With all that had happened in that short time, we hadn't even had a fire, only a drill.

"I wish that ugly old place had burned to the ground," I told Daddy later. "That building is just mean."

"You will be fine, honey," Daddy had assured me. "You have only one year there. Then you can transfer over to the newer building."

Although I made many friends that year, I was always afraid of the old, creaky school.

I finally got my wish. Several years later, the building burned down. I stood on a hill some distance away and watched hungry flames leap in and out of the windows. A heavy cloud of smoke hung over town that night as if to signal the end to an unhappy relationship. Early in the morning there was one last clanging of the heavy, cast-iron bell as the belfry weakened and finally fell, causing sparks and flames to shoot high into the air one last time.

As I stood there smelling the acrid smoke and watching as the flames settled deep into the bricks, it was as if I was bidding an unhappy, old maid aunt a final but relieved "farewell."

THE ROBBERY

"**H**ONEY, I WANT YOU TO BE MY CASHier. From now on, no one touches that cash register but you. Will you do that for me?" Dad asked.

"Ah, sure, Dad. Why not? But I don't know how to make change," I apologized.

"I'll teach you," he replied.

"But I might cheat you," I continued.

"If you make a mistake, it will be an honest one. Some people handling money in the restaurant now are cheating me on purpose. An honest mistake is only human."

Dad wove his confidence in me and his philosophy of honesty solidly together. It is a gift I have continued to appreciate.

"But Dad, I can't be a cashier, I'm only nine years old. Customers will laugh at me," I blurted out, frustrated.

"Don't worry about what people will do. Laugh with them, tease them, have a good time with them like you do now. Oh, they may laugh, but even the worst old skinflint in town won't cheat a child," he assured me.

In a few weeks I had become sure of myself for one so young. So it was with some surprise that Dad responded to a hastily written note from me late one Saturday night.

"Daddy, I think we have a problem," I said, matter-of-factly.

"I'm not surprised," he answered. "We've had the busiest day since we bought the café. If you have made mistakes, let's hope you cheated us and not our customers. I'll forgive you. They might not," he smiled wearily. He gently touched my chin. It was his way of saying I am proud of you without saying anything.

"Daddy, I think we are going to have a robbery. Two men have been in here several times tonight. Each time they pay they stare into the cash drawer."

Dad's face turned pale.

"Honey, if they tell you to hand over money, do it. They are committing a crime—they are scared. That makes them dangerous," he explained. "It is just money. They could kill you. No amount of money is as important as you are." Tears filled Dad's eyes as he finished.

Dad reached under the counter for a paper sack and filled it with bills. "I'm taking the largest amount to the kitchen. The bank is closed. They will not think to ask for this. Then I'm putting some more of it in a money sack," he said as he pushed a handful of twenty-dollar bills into a heavy canvas bank bag.

"I'm putting this bank money bag here under the counter," he explained. "Should they demand all your money, clean out the register drawer, then tell them there is more money in a bag under the counter. But don't reach for it. If you do, they could shoot you."

Dad looked so tired. "Whatever happens, keep calm. Don't shout, don't scream, and don't get scared. Just do what you are told. Okay?" Dad's blue eyes were grim now and his usually friendly face was hard. "If you see them again, call me. Okay?"

"Okay," I answered.

"And remember, you are the only little girl I've got. Be careful."

"Thanks, Dad."

Daddy's confidence gave me strength. He hugged me, took the sack full of bills, and went back to the kitchen.

We had the usual Saturday night rush. Farmers and
their families, who grew tired of their own food and
rarely ate out, did so on Saturday night. It was one way to
celebrate a long week's work together.

When I glanced out the large front window at my elbow,
what I saw made me weak. Two faces were pressed there
watching each time I opened the register drawer. Those
were the men. One glanced down the street; the other continued to stare into the drawer whenever I opened it.

My heart throbbed in my ears, and my mouth was
suddenly dry. I stared at the man's face unable to look
away. His eyes left the register and met mine. Daddy was
right. He was scared, but that open drawer gave him
courage. I swallowed hard as he reached for the door
handle.

Suddenly he was standing beside me.

"What time does your dad close?" he demanded. Perspiration glistened on his forehead.

"We close at 10:30 on Saturday nights, sometimes 11:00
if there is a crowd in town," I answered, suddenly aware
of a calmness inside in spite of my thundering heart.

"Ten-thirty or after, eh?" he asked.

"Yes, sir."

The restaurant was full with several people standing,
waiting.

"May I help you?" Suddenly I was aware of Daddy
quietly taking my place.

"Ah, no. I was just talkin' to your little girl," the man
stammered.

"I'll be glad to help you any way I can," Dad offered
more sharply than usual.

"Ah, yeah. Well, thanks," the man said as he bolted for
the door.

I sagged. "He is coming back, Daddy. He wanted to
know when we closed, and I told him."

"I could have guessed that. You watch for them while I call the police. But remember . . ."

". . . keep calm and give them the money," I interrupted.

"Exactly. And you are doing great." Dad tweaked my chin and was gone.

Several customers paid and chatted with me, never guessing what was happening. Dad made a phone call, nodded to me, meaning the police were coming, and returned to the kitchen.

That face was at the window again. Not knowing what else to do, I waved. "Might as well," I thought. "We are old buddies by now."

Then I watched the same two men appear again, cross the street and disappear around the corner building. A tumbleweed danced crazily down the street. The wind was getting up, coming off a cloud that had been slowly building in the southwest all afternoon.

It was getting late. A few people were lining up for the Saturday night late movie. Sometimes those lines stretched from the theater all the way around the corner. That happened on warm summer nights when a good first-run picture was showing. Tonight more people appeared interested in getting home. Cars raced down the street as distant thunder rumbled. Our street would soon be deserted.

As I stared, lightning flashed, and Main Street was blue-white with light. Two men—the same two—were standing just beyond the corner building across the street. As lightning flashed again, they turned toward our front door. It was a matter of time now. In trancelike stillness I continued to stare through the front window.

Once again, lightning struck nearby. Thunder cracked overhead, followed by a second lightning streak that cut a jagged pattern, then by eerie darkness. Thunder rolled again like a deep timpani drum, tightly keyed and vibrating.

During that last moment of blinding whiteness, two stark figures stood out against a rain-slick background, silhouettes of the two men staring blindly into the café. Suddenly the street was darker than ever. There were no lights. The electricity had gone off. Patches of lightning hopscotching through the clouds were our only lights.

I heard the front door squeak as it opened. Then, during a flash of lightning, the form of a man was outlined against the doorway. Blackness followed, thunder bellowed, and a man's voice called out, "Jeff, are you here?"

"Yes, we are," came Dad's reply.

"Has anything happened?" In a flash of lightning, I could see it was the sheriff as I sagged with tension. "Where are they?"

"Coming in behind you," Dad answered.

Thunder played a receding dance above us. "Hold it right there," shouted the sheriff.

The thunder boomed again, then became quiet. "You are under arrest," said the sheriff, stepping forward in a flash of lightning. Handcuffs clicked, and two figures stood still, hands behind their backs.

"This one has a loaded pistol. It's all right. I have it now," he announced, sliding the gun over toward the cash register.

From our dark vantage point, we could see the rain pouring down outside, the big drops playing staccato notes in the street. The thunder rumbled along some place further away now.

"Thanks a lot, sheriff" Dad said, shaking hands with his friend. Two handcuffed figures were led away as rain continued changing patterns on the wet pavement.

"Thanks, Dad. I was so scared," I said weakly, putting my arms around him.

"So was I," he returned, tweaking my chin once more. Then Mom joined us from the kitchen. We three stood there in the darkness, relieved and hugging each other.

A CHRISTMAS GIFT

AROUND THE CORNER AND DOWN THE street from the café was Appleton's Drugstore. Mr. Appleton had decorated every shelf in his store for Christmas. Tiny Christmas lights winked off and on, making dazzling spears of tinsel dance like rubies in the glass showcase. Rich brocade-and-satin boxes of cologne and petite perfume bottles peeked from folds of shiny fabric, contents turning from gold to burgundy and back to gold again. Each shelf held another luxurious set, but the most ornate box sat on the center one.

"It's that pink one in the middle, Daddy. See it?"

I danced up and down excitedly, tugging on my father's hand. Christmas holds a magic quality for nine-year-olds, and I had the Christmas spirit early.

Daddy bent down, taking a closer look. He was giving my suggestion careful consideration.

"Isn't it perfect?"

"It is very pretty, honey."

"Can we get it for her, Daddy?"

I could picture Mother's black eyes glowing with pleasure as she opened it. Daddy liked it, I could tell. But there was clearly something worrying him. He looked tired.

"It's awfully expensive," he said, almost too quietly.

"But we have got to give her something nice so she will know we love her."

"Mother knows that, sweetheart. But you do know what kinds of things she enjoys. Maybe we can find something like it that doesn't cost quite that much. It is beautiful, but sometimes we don't make that much money in a whole week." Daddy looked disappointed, but he gave me a reassuring hug.

"It's not fair. If God loves us so much, why are we so poor? Our pastor said God makes us rich, but we sure aren't!"

Now I was into my favorite line of questioning. This business of being poor was a sore spot with me.

"Being rich or poor doesn't depend on material things, sweetheart. We are rich, very rich. We have each other and Mother and Bob and Roy, and we love each other. Add to that our good health, and we are very rich. When we have all those things, we don't need lots of money."

When Daddy got philosophical, I got lost in his words. There was a gap in his thinking somewhere. My nine-year-old mind told me so.

Now, almost three weeks later, I had forgotten all about being poor. Tonight was Christmas Eve! Most of the stores were closing early so people could go home to be together with their families. I was back at Appleton's Drugstore to get a prescription for my little brother. I was the last customer, and while I was waiting, Daddy's words came back to me. He had found a gift for Mother very much like the one I had picked out, but it didn't cost as much. And although it was pretty, it wasn't in as nice a box. I had contributed two weeks of my allowance to it. We had wrapped it together one night and slipped it under our little Christmas tree at home. Daddy said shared surprises made Christmas special.

Suddenly a loud knock rattled the drugstore window. A well-dressed man and woman stood peeking through the glass and motioning for old Mr. Appleton to open the door. They obviously were strangers in town.

"We were closing early tonight. It's Christmas Eve," Mr. Appleton explained. "What can we do for you?"

"Yeah, yeah, Christmas! I'll make it worth your time, buddy," the red-faced man growled impatiently.

"The little woman is all upset about a Christmas gift. I told her she could buy anything she wanted, but she has some fancy notion about me picking it out. She gets crazy ideas in her head."

The lady was beautifully dressed. Her chestnut brown mink coat parted just enough to reveal a shimmering party dress like ones I'd seen in movies. But her face was tear-stained, and in spite of her glamourous appearance, she looked deeply hurt.

The couple stepped inside. The man swaggered up to the gift counter, a little too carelessly.

His voice seemed too loud as he slapped his hand down. The glass counter and contents inside danced crazily.

"Women! Ya' can't live with 'em, and ya' can't live without 'em. Whoever said that was one smart man."

He reached into his smooth leather jacket pocket and pulled out a small silver bottle, removed the lid, and took a long drink. "Give me a good drink, and I can celebrate any holiday ya' got!"

He walked around the little gift counter, crevices of his hand-tooled cowboy boots catching flashes from lights inside the perfume shelves.

"Well, come on," he snapped. "Make up your mind. It's getting later every minute, and this man said he wanted to go home."

The woman stood quietly, blinking back her tears.

"I wanted something you picked out for me. What it

costs isn't as important as it being your choice," she said. Tears on her lashes slipped down her cheeks and onto the mink coat.

"All right, all right. Let me see that box of stuff on the middle shelf there. That oughta make anybody happy."

He pointed to that pink satin-and-brocade box that still occupied the central place of honor.

"This is nice," Mr. Appleton said, carefully removing the much coveted box I had shown Daddy.

"It costs seventy-five dollars," Mr. Appleton continued apologetically. "Since it's Christmas and all, I might be able to take a few dollars off."

"I've got money, mister. More than enough." And with a flourish, he peeled off several large bills and tossed them onto the counter.

"While yer at it, tie it all up in some fancy paper and put a big bow on top." Turning, he asked, "Will that satisfy you?"

But his face wasn't happy when he said it, and he glared at the mink-clad figure that had moved away and was now staring miserably into the night.

Main Street was deserted as I walked home later. It was dark now, but Christmas lights still burned in windows of closed stores. Snow was beginning to fall, sifting like powdered sugar into cracks on the sidewalk.

An expensive motor roared behind me, and tires squealed as a nearly new car turned right. The couple from the drugstore was leaving town.

Wood smoke hung in the cold air as I dug my mittened hands deeper into my pockets. The paper wrapped around the prescription rattled, reminding me to hurry.

That couple certainly appeared to have money—plenty of it, I reflected. The new car, smooth leather jacket, and chestnut brown mink coat all were fresh in my mind.

There had been more money in that roll of bills than I had ever seen.

As the snow crunched beneath my feet, I felt very warm inside. Daddy's thinking might not be as confused as I had thought.

Maybe—just maybe—Daddy was right after all.

The Explosion

"**S**HUT THE DOOR! FLIES ARE GETTING IN!"

At mother's command, I closed the screen door to the café. Coming or going, flies were not of great concern to me at age ten.

Flies swarmed on the screen door and stuck there in early afternoon heat. White clouds billowed in the eastern sky, puffing up like marshmallows and promising much needed rain that probably wouldn't come. They were an empty promise of late August.

It was too hot to move, and everyone who could postpone their errands until later had done so. Only a few cars were parked on Main Street, and they were empty, windows down.

Swamp coolers purred in businesses that were open. Some stores had closed for the afternoon.

A gasoline truck pulled slowly down the street and backed into a gas station on the corner, and the driver began transferring gas from the truck to the storage tank. An old man sat on a bench shaded by the building.

Suddenly the ground rocked. Nearby windows shattered, and the truck exploded into a mountain of flame. A black, fiery stick on top of the transport gradually curled over, falling to the pavement. There was no sound from the still body that had once been a man. Someone inside the station raced to the crumpled form burning on the sidewalk, and willing hands reached out, grabbing the blackened, fiery thing and rolling it quickly in an effort to smother the fire. I watched in disbelief. The scene was like a movie.

The gasoline truck roared with hungry flames, quickly catching the station roof and the now vacant bench. The stench of burning flesh mixed with gasoline, burning wood, and hot rubber.

Shouting voices punctuated an escalating crescendo of the fire. "Fire department . . . help . . . hospital . . . emergency. . . ." the shouting voices increased as the fire roared.

"He is dead—has to be dead. Oh Gawd, the poor bugger!" The fire siren was screaming, raising its shrill voice to the highest pitch in its repertoire, over and over again.

Voices screamed as a crowd gathered on the street corner. Cars raced through the streets, horns honking as the volunteer fire department gathered at the fire station.

Precious minutes ticked past before a fire truck siren replaced the screech of the emergency alarm. Then a low-pitched whine joined the fire truck's siren.

"Barney's a-comin'," someone yelled.

"Good ole Barn. Always there when you need 'im."

The hearse turned the corner. There was no ambulance except those from Lawton and Oklahoma City, and in an emergency the only way to lay a man down was in the hearse. It belonged to the local funeral home and served several purposes as the situation demanded.

"He's dead all right."

"Yeah, cooked right through to the bone. Has to be."

I had wedged my way into the crowd. We stood at a respectful distance from the charcoaled mound lying on the sidewalk. The talk was quieter now that the fire was nearly out.

The truck was a blackened mass but still fairly well intact, except for a large gaping hole in the top. Water dripped and ran in ash-heaped rivers from the truck, gas pumps, and front of the station.

The hearse stopped near the truck driver's remains. A white-coated figure jumped from the passenger seat of the hearse, running to the crumpled form.

"The doctor must a-heard about it," someone said.

"Yeah, 'taint no use lookin' for no heartbeat. The poor bugger is dead, thank Gawd."

The doctor bent forward, stethoscope in hand. The crowd hushed. The blackened lump raised his head.

"Oh my Gawd, he's alive!"

The crowd moaned and stood transfixed, staring at the tragic, struggling figure on the ground.

Barney joined the doctor, body bag in hand. The doctor shook his head as the two leaned down.

"He's alive, and conscious," someone said.

"Ain't even screamin'."

"Probably cain't. Fire probably got his voice, too."

Barney rolled a gurney from the hearse and removed a white folded sheet from it. Gently, he and the doctor rolled the pathetic, blackened figure onto a sheet, then onto the gurney. A low moan filled the hushed silence, followed by a high-pitched scream. In spite of the August heat, I suddenly felt cold as chills chased each other up my back.

"He ain't lost all of his voice. He can still suffer out loud," someone remarked. The spectators stared, some through tear-filled eyes.

Barney and the doctor pulled the gurney gently toward the open doors of the hearse; other helpful hands reached out, but only Barney and the doctors touched the precious cargo. The moaning continued, punctuated by occasional sobs from the crowd.

Finally the hearse doors closed and the vehicle pulled away, proceeding slowly toward the hospital.

"The Methodist Church is open for them that wants to pray."

A hushed voice relayed the message across the café counter to Dad. He nodded his bald head in understanding. Their eyes never met.

"So is the Baptist Church and the Christian Church," added Dad.

The town's population had spoken in hushed tones all afternoon following the accident. Hospital updates ricocheted through town like bolts of lightning. The telephone operator was working overtime, calling key points along Main Street to update the victim's progress.

The driver was from a neighboring county. He had a wife and two small children, and there was no life insurance. Conoco Oil Company would pay the hospital and medical costs. It was their truck.

A benefit fund for the family was being collected at the newspaper office for those who wanted to give to the family. Several already had.

Those who visited the hospital reported the young man to be in excruciating pain. His wife was with him, and some church families had taken the little boys home.

Prayer groups met all night at local churches, staying from a few minutes to an hour or more. A few people sent flowers. Some sent fruit. But the local conversation had one theme: "How is he?"

He died early the next morning. Several people gathered to comfort the family as his wife and other family members left the hospital.

I watched the hearse as it rolled slowly down the street with the body. Cars stopped to let it pass, and men stood quietly, their hats in hand. The initial moment of horror had passed, but it would never be forgotten.

WORLD WAR II

WORLD WAR II BROUGHT RATIONING, EVEN to us. Sugar, gasoline, and silk hosiery were big on people's lists of "what I'm gonna get first when the war is over."

Mother's sense of humor hadn't been rationed, however, and she loved practical jokes. Her greatest contribution to the war effort was a good laugh.

When the usual "doughnut and coffee crowd" gathered one morning, Mother challenged a local grocery clerk with a good-natured bet.

"Joe, people are so ration-weary, I'll bet they would believe anything was rationed."

"Like what, Grace?"

"Oh, I don't know," she laughed. "Something silly. How about brooms?"

"Brooms? Why would the government need brooms?"

"They wouldn't. But I'll bet if I tell people broom corn is going to be rationed, you won't have a single broom left in stock by this time tomorrow. What do you wanna bet?"

"How about a couple of your homemade doughnuts and a cup of coffee?"

"That's fair. You're on."

They both laughed as Joe asked, "How will you spread the word, Grace? Put it on the radio?"

"Whisper," Mother giggled. "If you want people to believe something, whisper. You'll see."

So Mother began her campaign. Several times that day

she quietly asked someone if he or she had heard broom corn was being rationed.

"Broom corn?" the surprised return would come. "What fur?"

"Who knows," Mother would quietly answer. "Things don't have to make sense."

Soon after lunch, the phone began to ring.

"Just sold one fella four brooms and another two," laughed Joe. "I may have to pay for my doughnuts tomorrow after all!"

"Sure you will, Joe!"

During the afternoon, people on Main Street passed our front window carrying brooms. Some only had one, others two or three.

"Some of those folks are trying to corner the market," laughed Dad.

"I doubt it. They just plan to sell them later at a profit," Mother commented matter-of-factly.

Morning doughnut time was especially busy the next day, and in the rush Mother had forgotten her foolishness of the previous day.

"Joe, could you send over a couple of brooms when you get back to the store?" Mother asked innocently.

"I doubt it, Grace. We don't have any brooms. Nobody in town has any brooms. Remember our bet?"

"What bet?" She looked at him blankly.

"I owe you for two doughnuts and a cup of coffee this morning. Oh, and Grace, you did so well with brooms, why don't you start whispering about grocery stores. Ration those, and I'll retire soon!"

We felt the war in other, much more serious ways. Lack of cigarettes, sugar, and gasoline were minor inconveniences when compared to the young men who were called into the armed forces.

We all shared the loneliness families felt as one after another received their draft notices. When my cousin, Roy, got his letter of "greetings," the war came home to us.

Roy was a double cousin whose parents had died. Our family and home had become his, and he and I had played, argued, and gone through school just like brother and sister. Our greatest pastime was playing Monopoly. He usually won.

The day before Roy left for service, Daddy let us have one of the café tables all to ourselves. No matter how many people came in, we didn't have to take orders or give up our table. We had first rights to it because we were playing our last game of Monopoly together.

Customers came and went. A few of the regulars hung around watching me get beaten and listened to my screaming threats. But the game had a sad undertone, and more than once I saw Daddy silently wiping his eyes.

The next morning, Roy lined up at the Greyhound bus counter at the corner drugstore with several other young men. Then suddenly he was gone.

Daddy had been a cook in the army during World War I. "Didn't care much for cooking, son," he had told Roy, "but I figured somebody had to do it and I wouldn't die hungry."

When boot camp was over, Roy had applied for Cooks and Bakers School. They took him.

He was a good letter writer, and he wrote often. He filled us full of stories of his latest cooking catastrophes, and we laughed together at stories of his disasters.

As a navy cook, he was stationed in San Diego. The possibility of overseas duty was always present but not a thing we willingly faced. Each letter was proof he wasn't in the Pacific War Zone. Yet.

But one week there was no letter, nor was there one the

next week, which was followed by the longest month in my eleven-year-old life. Three months crawled by with no mail from him. We checked our post office box so often it would have needed a new paint job had it not been so old already.

"Grace, if that boy took my crazy advice and gets killed, it will be like I killed him myself."

"Jeff, it isn't your fault," Mother would answer. "You said what you thought was best."

The whole town knew Roy hadn't written, but most of them thought he had shipped out and hadn't been able to write.

Roy was prayed for at every church in town like all the other young men overseas or, worse, those missing in action.

Finally, it was difficult to discuss his mysterious disappearance. He had to be in the thick of the fighting. Guadalcanal maybe or Corregidor. Who knew?

Just when we were certain we would never see him again a letter came. I found it in the post office box that day as I was watching the mail being sorted. It was a ritual I had followed daily since he left.

When I recognized his handwriting on the envelope, I ran screaming all the way down Main Street. But I didn't open the letter. That was for Mom and Dad to do.

Dad's hands shook as he carefully cut it open. He didn't want to destroy one word of it.

Dear Uncle Jeff, Aunt Grace and that rotten Monopoly player.

I have been flipping pancakes from one end of San Diego Bay to the other on an LST training boat. It isn't easy, but I'm not overseas. We have been so busy we haven't been allowed to write. I hope you haven't worried too much because I can guess what you thought.

I'm gaining weight, and I'm fat and happy. I may get a
leave if this war is ever over. But, like you said, Uncle Jeff,
cooking isn't half bad, and I'm never hungry.
    Love you guys,
    Roy

The three of us hugged each other and cried the first
happy tears in more than three months!

Not all the boys were as lucky as Roy, nor was the
outcome of their long silences as humorous. Marvin was
one of those.

Marvin's dad owned and operated a barbershop three
doors up the street from Dad's café. Marvin was a serious
young man, yet he was always the "life of the Methodists'
young people's parties." He had finished college and
was attending a Methodist seminary when his "greetings" letter came. In fact, because he was older and un-
married, he was one of the first to go.

As Marvin made his rounds telling everyone good-bye,
he assured us all he would be fine. The army was taking
him as a chaplain, and he felt fortunate to be able to begin
his ministry where he was needed most.

Marvin's father, along with the pastor and the bulletins
at the First Methodist Church, kept us aware of where he
was. He was not allowed to give his exact position, but
his dad said he was on the front lines. That was where he
had requested to be because he would be needed.

Coming home from school one afternoon, I noticed the
barbershop was closed. As I opened the café door, Dad
quietly put the phone back on the hook. Then he answered my question.

"Marvin's father received a telegram from the War Department today. Marvin died in the line of duty on the
front lines in France." His words silenced all conversa-

tion at the counter. Heads bowed, coffee cups clanked on saucers. A couple of men silently wiped their eyes.

"He was the cream of the crop, such a kind, decent kid. He wanted out on the front lines where he could help others," Dad continued, eyes downcast.

"Chaplains ain't armed you know," someone at the counter added.

"That don't seem right, somehow."

"It ain't right. It just ain't. This whole war ain't right. Not when it takes the lives of our best young men."

"How is his father taking it?" That was the question on everyone's mind, and there was silence as we waited.

"Quietly," Dad answered. "He told me Marvin was doing what he wanted to do most, and he understood the risks. He was ready if this was the way he was to go."

There was a black crepe wreath on the barbershop door the next morning when I went to school. The memorial service was held at the First Methodist Church later that week. Marvin was buried in France.

Two months later a large box of fruit was delivered to the barbershop. Marvin had ordered it before he shipped out to France. Marvin's note said he was afraid he might not get his Christmas shopping done on the front lines.

He had been right. He hadn't.

THE BOX SUPPER

"REMEMBER PEARL HARBOR" MAY HAVE
been one of the most famous battle cries of modern history.
It certainly raised the patriotic heartbeat of America. It
sent our national metabolism into overdrive as the war
effort churned from a sputter of disbelief at the sneak
attack on Pearl Harbor, propelling us into a national frenzy
of reaction, a feverish peak of mobilization, and then all
out war. We would never forget, and neither would anyone else.

With the whirlwind speed of a mighty tiger stirred from
a midmorning nap, America awakened, scratched in disbelief, and retaliated. We would not forget, and the world
would forever remember the paybacks.

While men marched, quickly trained, and shipped out
to foreign shores, women tossed their aprons on the kitchen
tables and left home to staff the factories that built the
planes, ships, and fire power their men would carry. The
famous battles of World War II were fought while we built
the weapons at home.

Then we reached deep within our pockets to pay the
price it would cost. We bought war bonds out of our
checks—weekly or monthly—because freedom and liberty meant more to us than our bank deposits. We marched
in parades and held rallies. At every level the activity was
decorated in red, white, and blue. One of the most down-

home efforts to sell bonds was the box supper, usually held at the local high school.

The box supper originally had been a shy man's way of paying a dollar or two to buy a frilly, decorated box containing some of his favorite dishes cooked by his local sweetheart. It was an innocent social custom that could result a few months later in an engagement and a marriage. But with the national battle cry of the war, this sleepy, social custom changed in appearance and atmosphere.

In contrast, the box supper of World War II became a noisy, vital revenge on the high cost of waging war and paying its debt. The once frilly little powder fluff tops that served as coverings for deep-dish pecan pies, southern fried chicken, and potato salad now sported warship likenesses of the *Arizona* with "Remember Pearl Harbor" signs attached to the upturned bow disappearing through make-believe ocean-froth netting.

Bidding no longer timidly began at fifty cents. Instead, a professional auctioneer pledged his services to the war effort for the night, seized the historically decorated box and, hoisting it high into the air, shouted full volume, "Do I hear a twenty-five-dollar bond? Now do I hear a fifty?"

"I bid a thousand," someone shouted, and the bidding war was on. The money flowed as the war effort gathered steam and we citizens had a heartfelt obligation to "back our boys."

As a budding teenager, my problem was not in selling the box but in getting young men in my teenage range to buy it. The teen crowd had less money than the adults and older generations. And, of course, there were no young adult males ages seventeen to thirty. They were all away fighting the war.

Kids, as they always have, loved sweets and junk food such as it was in those days. "Mother, put in lots of potato chips, some candy bars, and things kids like," I'd plead. But she assured me when it came to food she "knew what people liked to eat." The box was filled with fried chicken, banana nut cake, potato salad, pea salad, and sometimes even chess pie. It weighed a ton, which was another embarrassment.

"Boys, if you're hungry, buy this box. If all I'm lifting here is food, you'll have enough for all next week!" the auctioneer shouted and every old, fat man in hearing distance licked his lips to bid. My partner was bald, fat, and at least forty. The closest I ever came to an even slightly romantic encounter, something box suppers were supposed to have been, was when one man bought several boxes, rather than one. He had an unusually fine cotton crop that fall, so he did his share in buying war bonds. At the last minute—my box was one of the last ones sold due in part to its weight—the auctioneer pleaded for a final bid of $2,000 for all the remaining boxes. He got the bid and asked each of us to find someone hungry to eat with.

My partner was a very hungry nine-year-old redhead. At the ripe old age of twelve, I found nothing about him that was romantic. All we had in common were our appetites.

So the great social custom of the yearly box supper at the local schoolhouse of the 1930s became one of the feverish fundraisers for war bonds of the forties as Main Street went to war, financing and supporting with rallies, parades, and the old country custom of box suppers.

CHARLIE

HIS WRINKLED FACE AND WHITE HAIR framed twinkling blue eyes and a ready smile. He was nearly always dressed in old blue denim overalls and a floppy old hat, but those faded work clothes covered one of the warmest hearts in town. He was my friend Charlie.

Charlie owned the local "fixit shop" down the alley from my parents' café. He repaired toasters, waffle irons, and other small appliances, things we usually throw away today. He sometimes sold some of them "second-hand." His shop was merely an effort to stay busy during his retirement years. However, his pastime, which was much of the time, was an ongoing domino game over at the local jail.

It was a short walk to the café for coffee and a couple of meals a day, but the distance and the weather never mattered. We could set our clocks by Charlie's arrival.

He was a great pal of mine, and we shared a lot of good times. One of our favorite moments occurred with the onset of summer when the corn got ripe. We greeted that season with our annual corn-eating marathon. It was usually announced by the almost formal arrival of Charlie carrying an overstuffed sack full of fresh "roasting ears" over his back.

Mother would shuck the ears and slip them into a pan of boiling water that was lightly salted and sugared. Boiled, those ears were the crunchiest, sweetest treat this side of heaven.

Charlie and I would take our places at the café counter, both of us armed with a plate, plenty of real butter, knives, empty plates to put the empty cobs on, and a bundle of napkins between us.

Charlie would roll up his sleeves, and Daddy would tie dishtowels around our necks. Then we would begin to chomp corn in earnest. The race had nothing to do with speed—just the number of ears consumed and by whom.

Usually we were surrounded by a healthy number of oldsters who had nothing else to do. Of course, Mother and Daddy and anyone who happened to be working that day stopped to become part of the cheering section.

As usual, Charlie and I rose to the occasion. Lavishly buttering our corn, we leaned into our work. The fresh ears were juicy, sweet, and heavily buttered, and we were equal to the task before us. Spurred on by the delicious crunchiness of the food in front of us, we inspired each other with well-placed comments. These mild insults covered a spectrum of subjects, from the fear we felt for our opponent's health to references to last year's less than stunning performances. As the stack of naked cobs grew, so did our verbal battle.

"I've heard of little 'uns a-eatin' so much corn it dun went and turned 'em yellar," Charlie might say.

"Speakin' of health, maybe you need to stop before you die of indigestion. A bad case of stomach cramps could kill somebody as old as you are," I'd tease.

"Naw, corn is good for the body," he would argue. "I would't a-lived to be this old if it hadn't a-been for the fine corn they grow around here. I was born on corn, raised on corn, and I'll die on corn, the Lord willin'."

"Yeah, and real soon too if you don't stop eating. Aren't you even a little bit full?" I pleaded, hopefully. But the contest wouldn't end until neither of us could eat another bite. Then the cobs would be counted, and one or the other of us would be declared the winner. However, the corn eating never really stopped because in our continuing teasing, references would be made to the other person's less than sterling performance in last year's tournament.

I never remember getting sick, and if Charlie did he never mentioned it. However, there was one incident that completely eclipsed all of the others. This one didn't concern corn.

After more than two years of saving my paltry allowance of thirty-five cents a week, I finally unlocked my little tin bank and dumped the contents onto the counter. Not all of those nickels, dimes, pennies, and quarters were really mine. Charlie and numerous other members of the domino set would pay me for their coffee at the cash register, then ask the magic question:

"Are ya' still a-savin' fur that bicycle?" They would then contribute their leftover change, which was never very much, to my growing dream of "someday."

Over and over I had counted the contents of that little bank, but there was never quite enough. This year, however, I had found a beautiful secondhand red-and-white Western Flyer for sale, and I was holding my breath.

I stared at it through the café window as Daddy and I stacked pennies in stacks of ten each and placed them carefully in one-dollar piles. The setting sun glistened on the shiny steel handlebars as that glorious creation rested majestically on its own kickstand. I could feel my heart beating against my chest as Daddy counted, "thirteen . . . fourteen dollars and seventy-five cents."

I cringed. The man selling the bicycle had asked for more money than that, but thirty-five cents a week doesn't mount up very fast when all of one's necessities have to be purchased from that small amount. One of those absolute "musts" was a ten-cent ticket every Saturday to witness Roy Rogers or Gene Autry bring law and a decent way of life back to the open range. Missing that weekly highlight would have been unthinkable. Those two men were my heroes, and I was going to grow up and marry both of them.

"Would you be willing to take fourteen dollars and seventy-five cents for your bicycle?" Dad negotiated.

"Well, my son had wanted more. He is going off to college, and he should take it with him. But you know how kids are."

I held my breath. I had to have that bicycle. I had to. But what if I didn't have enough money? I closed my eyes and prayed. I knew God heard our prayers, but I wasn't really sure if that included bicycles. Oh well, I had to have it. I had nowhere else to turn. Just before I got to the final part of offering my life for full-time overseas missionary service, the deal was made!

Daddy scooped up all the change into one of the bank sacks and handed over fourteen crisp, one-dollar bills: "Thirteen . . . fourteen dollars, and three quarters make it seventy-five cents!"

That beautiful dream standing so proudly on our front sidewalk was m-i-n-e. The dream of someday was now, today!

I could not keep still. "Can I ride it now, Daddy, can I please?" I begged.

"Well, it is getting late and your mother doesn't want you out after dark, but go ahead. Whatever you do, be back before dark. Promise me," Daddy pleaded.

"Oh, I will, I will," I squealed, running out the door and to my dream ride around the block for the first time.

As the late evening breeze touched and lifted my hair, my heart soared. This is the way heaven will be, I thought.

My first full stop was in front of Charlie's Fix-it Shop. He was just closing the door for the day as I glided gracefully to a stop in front of him.

"Charlie, look! I have that bicycle, finally," I announced triumphantly, dropping off so he could get a full view of its awesomeness.

"Isn't it a beauty?" I squealed.

"It sure is," he agreed, admiringly running his hands over the bright handlebars.

"I can't believe it's real! And I *really* can't believe it belongs to me!"

"Oh it's a beauty, all right!" Charlie walked slowly around it, getting a full view from all sides. His admiration was complete. Finally he took the handlebars and, placing his foot on the pedal, slapped the leather seat with his other hand. "How about lettin' me go for a little spin?"

"What? You want to ride my bicycle? You can't do that. Bicycles are for kids," I countered.

"I'm a kid," he laughed, looking younger than I could ever remember. With that, he swung his leg over the seat and, getting his balance, rode away into the gathering dusk.

I stood there in the middle of the street, my mouth wide open in disbelief. My bicycle was gone, and so was Charlie. I stared toward the corner where he had turned. He wasn't coming back. He really wasn't ever coming back. In my eleven-year-old imagination, I knew I'd never see him or my new bike again. Tears gathered in my eyes and streamed down my face. Charlie had ridden my beautiful new bicycle right off into eternity, and he wasn't coming back, not ever. Those few seconds turned into what seemed like hours of total anguish.

I began running hard down the alley to the café, crying all the way. The tears flooded my eyes until seeing where

I was going was nearly impossible in the gathering darkness.

As I reached the end of the alley, I saw the front window bathed in light and realized Daddy had already turned on the lights. The streetlights were coming on. I should have been home, but not like this.

I rushed into the café shouting, "Mother, Daddy, my bicycle has been stolen, and I'm never going to get it back." The sobs choked me, making me cough.

"Your what?" Dad asked in disbelief. "What happened? Did you fall? Are you hurt?"

Mother rushed up in verbal full swing, "Honey, are you all right? I knew I shouldn't let you go. That bicycle has no light. It is dark already, and she isn't used to riding it yet. Did you fall? Are there any broken bones? You shouldn't be riding at night—now Jeff, I told you—"

"Charlie stole my bicyle," I howled. "Just got on it and rode right off. I watched him—"

People at the counter began gathering around to pick up all the details.

"What did you say?"

"Charlie *who* stole your bicycle?"

"Charlie Aston," I loudly confirmed.

"*Charlie* stole your bicycle?" Dad said, trying not to laugh. The picture of what had happened was finally taking shape in his mind.

"Yes, he did. He just grabbed that bicycle and just took off right down the street. Just like that!" Fresh tears gushed with that proclamation.

The people gathered around began to laugh. "That ole rascal!"

"What do ya' think a that!"

"That old scamp would do anything for a laugh. Anything."

"I hardly think he will get far," laughed Dad. "He just celebrated his eightieth birthday!"

Just then, in the circle of light from our front window, a figure rode slowly into sight. With great care he dismounted a red-and-white bicycle, placed its kickstand, and reached for our front door. It was Charlie.

Slightly out of breath and fully flushed with the recent excitement, Charlie said, "Did Norene tell you I rode her bicycle? Yep, rode that beauty right around to the jail and showed those old coots *my* new bicycle. Nearly killed 'em. None of them could do it, by golly! I showed 'em all!" He proudly laughed, and everyone but me laughed with him.

Daddy and Mother joined the other customers in congratulating Charlie on his flight past the jail.

Daddy turned to me. "Charlie has really pulled a good joke on you this time. It will take quite a payback to equal that one!"

Slowly I had calmed down. That was pretty funny, come to think of it. I'd never be able to eat enough corn to top it.

"Oh, and honey," Daddy smiled at me, "if the only people who steal that bike are eighty or above, I don't think you'll ever have to worry about losing it!"

As the impact of his statement hit me, I grinned with a big sigh of relief.

THE OIL WELL

MOTHER WAS THE COOK, AND THE CAFÉ was her unique outlet. Daddy had accepted it as an alternative for supporting the family when the industrial revolution outdistanced the mules that had pulled his plows.

The depression left no money to buy farm machinery, and by the late thirties a farmer with only a team of mules could not make a living for a family of three, no matter how thrifty. So in its own way my family marketed one of the most creative skills it had: Mother's southern cooking.

Dad packed away his blue-striped overalls and put on an apron. Together, side by side, he and Mother served her rolls, deep-fried chicken, and chicken-fried steak. The café provided a much better living in the forties and fifties than the farm ever had with no modern equipment, but Dad loved the land and always dreamed of "going back to it one day."

"Your mother is happy here," he would often say "but I'm just the chief cook and bottle washer." Then a far-away look would cross his face as he reminisced about the smell of freshly turned sod on an early spring morning or the crisp quiet of late fall along a creek bottom.

On rare times away from the café, Mother would pack an old iron skillet, a gallon can, coffee, bacon, and potatoes and the three of us would picnic near a picturesque creek bottom out in the country somewhere. During those infrequent outings, Mom and Dad would walk the creek and dream Dad's dream of putting together enough money to buy a farm this time—not rent as before—and live the simple, fulfilling life of the land: a few chickens, a cow or two, and the unending tasks that entailed.

Dad searched the ads, and again and again we looked at farms—farms with shacks, houses, or no houses at all. Each time, in our imaginations we moved in, but somehow none of them were ever right until a farm south of town came on the market.

This farm was 160 acres or 360 acres—I don't remember which—but it had a house Mother and I loved. There was a barn, which needed some fixing, but best of all it had a creek that actually had water running through it. My little brother, Bob, was just a baby, so we visualized him fishing there as he grew older. Bob needed that farm more than we did, we reasoned, because in town he had no place to play. Here he would. We had finally found our farm. We were in love.

Dad feverishly figured his assets. The café should sell for this much, and he would try to be reasonable with his estimate. The building could bring as much as this figure, and again he would conservatively scale back the figures, hoping it would bring more. Finally, there was the savings account. He had good credit. He could borrow, and again he was conservative in his estimate. But no matter how he figured, there was not enough money and credit and realistic dreams to make it all come true.

The price of the entire farm package was $25,000 or perhaps $40,000. Whatever the figure, it was "more money than we would ever see in this lifetime." Money was something we just didn't have, and the amount— whatever it was—was the most money I could remember ever wishing we had all at one time! Dad dreamed and talked and walked the floor late at night when he should have been resting for the heavy day ahead. He made several trips to the Farmer's National Bank with his carefully scripted notes of assets, ideas, and crop forecasts, but it was all for nothing.

One day the banker called to tell us the farm was being sold to someone else, someone who had the borrowing power to realize the dream we had all held so dear.

That weekend we packed the iron skillet, coffee, boiling can, potatoes, and bacon and made our final visit to our favorite picnic spot on the creek bottom. As the little stream gushed across the white river rock at our fingertips, we ate our last meal surrounded by the dream that would never be.

Each of us said good-bye in our own way. Bob and I played in the water while Mom and Dad walked away to be together. When they returned, Mother had been crying and Dad was wiping his eyes. As I recall, although the smell of coffee, potatoes, and bacon on a campfire filled the fall air, none of us ate very much. Finally, we cleaned up our mess, put out our campfire for the last time, and drove away. None of us mentioned the farm again. It was gone.

Just over a year later, I rushed home from school one afternoon to find Dad looking out the café window with "that wistful look" on his face again. But his face spoke volumes more of disappointment and disbelief.

"Norene, they struck oil on the farm last week!" I didn't need to ask what farm or where. I knew.

"Their first check was for nearly $100,000. I guess God knows I wouldn't know what to do with money if He gave it to me." For a moment tears welled in his eyes. Then he put his arms around me and gently rested his head on mine.

"Aw, Daddy, if we had bought that farm, we wouldn't have struck oil."

"What do you mean?"

"With our luck, all of the oil would've come in on the

farm next to it, and we would still have been dirt poor!" I explained, looking up at him while giving him a much needed hug. We both laughed together.

"You're probably right, honey," he answered. "You're probably right!"

DISCIPLINE AND THE CLOCK GAME

"Son," DADDY SAID, "HOW IS A POOR hard-working old man supposed to get up with no alarm clock?" As he picked up the clock, the clatter from inside was unmistakable. The little clock case was full of moving parts, but none of them were connected.

Daddy tried to look stern, but his eyes danced, a smile tickling the corners of his mouth.

"See clock sing!" babbled the three-year-old boy as he clapped his hands and giggled contagiously.

"That clock won't sing anymore. It can't," Dad said, trying to maintain his serious air.

"Clock sing, Daddy," continued the bouncy little fellow. "That clock sings. It does Daddy, and I pix!"

"Oh, you fixed it all right, and as usual you did a grand job of it. Not one part is left joined to another. This is the third clock you have taken apart lately, son. Now what are Mother and I going to do?"

"Bobby boy pix it some," the little boy squealed while he danced around in circles, his face wreathed in smiling accomplishment.

"This is the third time Mother and I have been late opening up the café because our clock no longer works. The second time I put it up on that shelf, and this time I hid it under the bed. Now son, Daddy is going to have to

70

get stern with you. I know you must know by now to leave my clock alone, so the next time it happens, your mother will have to punish you."

Daddy was tired and his frustration showed, but each time he looked at the bubbly little boy that was his son he looked proudly helpless.

Most of the time we were putty in the little boy's hands, but there were times when stronger measures had to be taken. As usual, Daddy was happy to offer Mother's services. Her black eyes could snap fire, and so could her little willow switches. That had always been true in my case. The sentence was deferred to Mother. Daddy would need to be away for some convenient reason, and while he was gone, Mother would guide me in my selection of a small, flexible willow switch. We would place it in a prominent place where I could see and admire it for several days. Finally, in succeeding days, I'd manage to do that one final thing. The switch would sting my legs briefly. I'd cry because it hurt, but most of all because my pride was hurt. Then the period of punishment would be over, and my slate of past misdemeanors would be clean. I could start all over again, and this time I would know I was going to be good forever after.

With Bob, it turned out to be a different story. Mother balked.

"Jeff, I took care of Norene's punishments, but Bob is a boy. This time you will have to take care of it yourself. I know you are softhearted, but a boy must grow up respecting his father because his father is his example. Besides, I've done my time," she argued.

Daddy was stuck. He did his duty as the chief disciplinarian, but he obviously hated it.

Mother always assured me the switching was going to hurt her more than it hurt me. I never was convinced.

But Bob never really left the clocks alone, or his toys

with moving parts. Radios were another catastrophe—if two parts fit together, he needed to see how they looked apart. Truly amazing, though, he soon put them back together again and they worked.

Bob's ability to assemble things got lost somewhere as he grew older. Perhaps instructions confused him. The "join A to D and bend back to C" made no sense. Maybe the reassembly ceased to make sense. Who knows? But gradually the heap of unassembled toys and clocks, and things we no longer recognized, grew to unbelievable proportions. It seemed he was more intrigued with the unassembled parts than with the item all in one piece. Not all the parts were wasted, though. Pieces of things turned up later in his creative play.

Years later as an adult, he was completely baffled by items that had to be put together. Visiting his family one time after he was grown, I noticed a small mountain of twisted steel in his back yard.

"What is *that?*" I asked.

"An answer to fervent prayer," he answered so seriously I suspected foul play. "I found an excellent tool shed on sale at Sears, bought it not realizing it came in a box with a mountain of nuts and bolts accompanied by a short novel of 'instructions.' After weeks of wrestling with it, my back yard looked like a World War II battlefield. There was only one thing to do: pray for a tornado. My prayer life must have increased several-fold, and finally we had a hard wind. There is the final result! With what I collected on damages, I can now afford to buy a tool shed fully assembled."

He seemed sincerely pleased with himself.

"But you could put things back together when you were little," I argued.

"If I ever had that ability, I don't remember it. But you know, every time I attacked the parts of that shed, I remembered all Dad's clocks. That must have been one of the reasons that poor man lost his hair!"

On a return visit the following year, I admired Bob's new, wooden tool shed.

"I couldn't stand the sight of another steel one," he explained. "It represented too much pain."

THE CONFRONTATION

"SHE DONE WENT AND DONE ME WRONG again. . . ." the words from the country-western song howled up and down the street. The café door was open, and the nickelodeon was occasionally turned full blast in spite of Daddy's efforts to keep the volume turned down. I could hear that country-western music in my sleep, to say nothing of the haunting lyrics. Those always sad laments were a long way from my favorite fare.

Loud music was a pet peeve of Daddy's. He was a quiet man and exceptionally patient, but it was a mistake to ever think of him as a milquetoast. Daddy could quietly stand his ground with anyone, and once he did, he was most persuasive. He would logically sketch out the situation and he and the person involved eventually reached the same conclusion—his—for the good of all.

Daddy didn't make these "suggestions" selfishly or to embarrass anyone, or even for the sake of winning an argument. As he viewed his own problem, he was able to see the bigger picture. Daddy usually took the philosophical approach, and that was true in the case of the nickelodeon. It was just an ongoing problem that needed solving several times each year.

Townspeople knew and appreciated our rules on noise. The teenage crowd respected Dad and knew better than to cross him. However, the majority of offenders were people who were not acquainted with him. When they turned up the volume button, they were opening a new chapter in their lives—one they would never forget. These transgressors were usually strangers from out of town, including truck drivers just stopping for a break in a long haul to somewhere. Sometimes they had been drinking as well.

"I may be mistaken, but I believe you turned up the volume on the nickelodeon," Dad would quietly begin, right after he turned it down.

The man facing him was much larger and more muscular than Dad. His face was flushed, suggesting the presence of alcohol, and his attitude was defensive. "Yeah, so what? If I cain't hear it, I ain't playin' it," the offender retorted.

"You, of course, must make that choice for yourself," Dad advised. "We run a quiet business here. Many of our customers come here to talk as well as to enjoy the music. We always try to respect their wishes."

"Oh, yeah? Well, if I cain't hear it, I cain't hear it! So I turned it up. Whattayah plan to do about it?"

"Ask you to respect my request and that of my other customers," Dad answered in his quiet, controlled voice, but his eyes and jaw were firmly set.

The two had reached an impasse that had danger written all over it. Such a time was Dad's forte.

"However, I believe you have a bigger problem than that. Now, I may be mistaken—I certainly have been before—but you appear to have been drinking."

"Sure, I've had a drink. So what are you gonna do about it? What I drink and don't drink is my business, mister!"

"It is my business when it is in my home," Dad answered firmly, never moving his eyes from the truck driver's face. Then he placed his hand lightly on the man's shoulder and leaned toward him as if to take him into his confidence.

"You see, I have my wife and children in here, too. I have no other choice. So I must ask you to behave in here just as if you were in the living room of my home. I'm sure you understand what I mean. You are our guest, but just as surely as I would never allow a guest who had been drinking heavily to come into my home, so I must ask you to do the same here."

"Hey, man. What are you tryin' to say?" The truck driver was still defensive but had lowered his voice.

"I'm saying that I can't allow you to come in here when you are drinking. I know you understand my problem."

"Are you a-tellin' me to leave? If you don't need my business, I sure as hell don't need this place." With that parting remark, he lurched toward the door.

Dad stood quietly watching him go. Then he turned and walked back into the kitchen.

A couple of weeks later, a stranger came into the café, walked to the cash register, and looked at me. Finally he said, "Are you the owner's little girl?"

"Yes, I am."

"Is your dad here?"

"Yes, he's in the kitchen."

"Would you get him for me? I need to talk to him."

"Yes, wait here," I answered as I headed toward the kitchen. "Daddy, some strange man is here to see you."

As Dad came from the kitchen drying his hands on a towel, the stranger walked toward him with his hand extended.

"My name is Blair, Richard Blair," he began, shaking hands with Daddy.

"It's my pleasure, sir. What can I do for you?"

"I came back to say 'thank you.' You woke me up the other day when you refused me service. My drinking has sure gotten outta hand since my wife and I separated. I'm on another long haul from the West Coast, and I'd appreciate it if you would allow me to eat here. I'm not drinking today."

"We would be happy to have you," Dad replied. "Sit anywhere. My wife and I have just finished cooking up some fine chicken-fried steak. I could recommend that. My wife's yeast rolls just came out of the oven, too. Have a seat, and we will have your food in just a few minutes. Oh, meet my daughter. She is my cashier, but sometimes she waits tables, too."

The man solemnly shook my hand and sat down at the counter. I placed a napkin, water, and utensils in front of him. In only a few minutes, Daddy returned with freshly fried steak, complemented with one of Mother's "ovensized" yeast rolls, mashed potatoes, creamy steak gravy, and fresh corn. From the looks of the clean plate when Mr. Blair finished, the food was good.

"Those rolls are the best I have ever tasted," he said as he paid me for his meal at the register.

Dad reappeared from the kitchen. He stepped around the counter and shook hands with the man.

"Come back anytime."

"Thanks, I will. And Mr. Murphey—thank you for letting me come back."

"It was my pleasure," answered Dad.

"No sir, it was mine!"

Mr. Blair came often after that, but not when he was drinking. Over the years Daddy had numerous confrontations—often over the nickelodeon volume—but most of them turned out just as the one with Mr. Blair. The surprising thing is that not one of the people Dad refused service to ever attempted any physical harm. Either they didn't come back at all or, like Mr. Blair, came when they were not drinking.

Daddy made lots of friends. No matter what the people had done, he respected them. They might not be welcome today, but they would be when their behavior changed. Had Dad been bold, brash, or self-serving, the outcome could have been entirely different. But in his calm, humble way Daddy approached problems without making anyone angry. Or if he did, they didn't stay that way long.

THE FIRST
BAPTIST CHURCH

JUNE, JULY, AND AUGUST WERE HOT. Really hot. Temperatures often soared to 100 degrees Fahrenheit and stayed there, sometimes for a month or more without a break. With no air conditioning, hot weather always ushered in summer revival meetings.

The Baptists could be depended on to be dramatic. Hell was a popular pulpit topic then, along with Judgment Day. Hell, Judgment Day, and hot weather consolidated forces to remind everyone to "get right with the Lord."

One summer the Baptist evangelist outdid himself. He "packed the pews" with people, many of whom hadn't been in church in years. Then he heaped hell's brimstone curb high for two full weeks. He scared such a record number of people into heaven that the board of deacons met and called him as the permanent pastor.

The Christian Church and Methodist Church had summer revivals, too, but those Baptists opened up hell's gate and scooped on the coal. Usually, when the two weeks were up, the townsfolk heaved a sigh and went back to normal, routine sinning. But not this year. This time nobody rested.

The community had a Baptist William Jennings Bryan for a preacher. He could be heard whether sinners were in church or not. He could be understood outside on the sidewalk whether windows were open or shut. So he gathered two crowds: pew sitters and the sidewalk standees across the street.

The sidewalk crowd was a dozen or so old-age pensioners who gathered regularly to place bets on an ongoing domino game at the city jail. The jail served well as a domino parlor since it had only one cell used by the town drunk when he couldn't make it home nights.

In the summertime, the elderly widowers in their overalls, faded blue denim shirts, and sweat-soaked straw hats moved the domino tables outside. It was then, after they moved outside, that the voice from the church caught their attention. The sermon content was of no consequence. None of them attended church anyway. Instead, this fire-breathing sideshow offered an exciting, new betting target.

With news that the "fancy fireslinger" was staying on, the dedicated domino crowd suspended its marathon games during church services in favor of more fertile betting possibilities. Some local businessmen capitalized on a good thing and had wooden benches built across from the church. Business names were blazed across those bench backs for advertising, but they served as bleachers for the growing elderly sidewalk crowd.

"By Gawd, he was sure a-burnin' it this mornin', warn't he?"

"Yep, that were a round trip to hell with nary a ticket needed."

"Hey Mac, how many times air ya' sayin' hell 'ill break loose tonight?"

"Aw Ed, I ain't bettin' ya this time. I nigh onto lost my shirt and shirttail both last Wednesday night."

"Come on. Be sportin' now. If he stirs up hell twenty-five times the first half-hour, I'll relieve ya' of that Bull Durham tobaccer in yer pocket."

"I'll not say twenty-five. I'll raise ya' five and throw in a new pack of cigarette papers to boot."

Then the service began. While the new preacher laid blistering blocks of brimstone end to end and back to back, the peanut gallery on the benches kept score.

"Twenty-nine, thirty! That did 'er! I'm out!"

With the beginning of "Just As I Am" ringing up and down Main Street, bets were tallied and money exchanged.

By the final "amen," both congregations were dismissed. Everyone went home. Thirty minutes later the church was dark, the streets deserted.

When these elderly pensioners came into the café, I mentioned to Daddy two or three times what they were doing outside the church, but he said it wasn't nice to talk about people that way.

That preacher stayed two years. The congregations gained several members, and attendance was good. The bench crowd changed only in bad weather. Excitement never waned, except once.

The preacher got wind of his second congregation and visited the bleacher crowd one night. But instead of welcoming the attention, the oldsters were miffed. When the handshaking was over, the little crowd dispersed rather than "come inside." They returned only gradually over the following two weeks in twos and threes. Their sermon interest was in a different direction, and it was a good bet that preacher never knew what it was.

JUDGMENT DAY

SINCE THE WORLD WAS COMING TO AN
end at eleven o'clock, nobody had studied for the seventh-
grade health test. The prophecy was the handiwork of a
well-known radio preacher, and everyone in town was
talking about it, especially the kids at school.

The tension had been building for weeks. Most of the
preachers in the community had dealt with the topic
from once to many times over the last several Sundays.
Most of them had agreed that "we were living in the last
days" and that there had been "wars and rumors of wars
and earthquakes in diverse places." Well, we'd had our
share of tornado scares, and the boll weevils had been
especially heavy this year, if that qualified.

So as the fateful day neared, we postponed things we
didn't like doing because Judgment Day was Monday,
April 10, at 11:00 A.M., anyhow.

That morning at school our lives were measured in
hours rather than days. Doomsayers occupied center
stage in the girls' restroom. As we combed our hair in
preparation for first period, the conversation was typical
of what was being said on Main Street.

"Daddy said he thought the world could end just like
that," said one girl, snapping her fingers.

"Yeah, our pastor says all the signs of the times point
to it."

"I'm scared!"

"Me too," someone added.

"We've been studying Revelation at church and it says. . . ."

The conversations washed toward the dramatic pronouncements of what a variety of denominations had to say about the radio prophecy.

Finally I injected my Dad's comment of the night before. "Daddy said it was the end of the world for somebody every day, so he wasn't going to worry about it."

"Norene, you are just no fun. You know what the Bible says."

"Yeah, and I can't imagine it happening today!"

"So did you study for the health test?"

"No," I replied guiltily. "Who needs it when that period doesn't begin until 11:30?"

"Exactly. And what do you have at eleven o'clock today?"

"Home Economics."

"Imagine meeting your Maker over a sewing machine."

For the most part, the idea was almost a joke, but enough talk had been generated to catch people's curiosity and cause a lot of comments. It was enough to blow a seventh-grader's mind.

When Daddy had discovered how worried I was about the prophecy, he had taken time to sit down and read to me from the Bible. "See, honey," he said, finishing Matthew 24, "not even the angels in heaven know when Judgment Day will be, so neither would some well-meaning man on the radio." I felt better after that.

The morning was stormy with occasional rain, but 10:30 brought a typical April thunderstorm. As the clouds darkened the sky and the thunder grumbled, that last thirty-minute countdown intensified.

Our minds were not on the "garments" we were making, and our hearts were not in our work. As the minutes ticked away and the hands of the clock neared eleven, the storm moved in to provide plenty of dynamics in sound and setting. Just as the clock hands reached zero hour, a bolt of lightning streaked through the clouds to its point of impact directly outside the window. Simultaneously, an ear-splitting roar of thunder shook the building until the windows clattered in their frames.

"This is it!" someone screamed. We all dived underneath the heavy sewing tables. Several girls cried while others covered their heads with their arms. My knees were no longer strong enough to hold up my body, and I crumbled under the table with the others. Seconds passed while the storm rolled over us and rain lashed the windows in furious sheets. Then the storm gradually diminished as rain continued in a steady downpour and the thunder crept farther away, still mumbling grim reminders.

"Girls, you can come out from under the tables," instructed the commanding voice of our teacher. "The Lord didn't come, although I wondered there for a minute. I'd say he left a pretty good calling card!"

No one laughed. The violence of the storm at the moment the clock reached the magic hour had been close enough to reality for all of us. Class was dismissed.

Eleven-thirty came, and we were not ready. Soaked from racing back to the main building, we sat in wet, repentent silence as our health teacher passed out the tests. Finally someone held up his hand and asked the obvious question on all of our minds.

"Do we have to take the test today? I don't think any of us are ready!"

With a straight face the teacher faced the class. "Yes, you must take the test! It's Judgment Day, remember?"

A Worship Experience

"Son," Daddy began, "we are going to church to listen to the preacher this morning. This time you are to sit still and let us worship. Do you understand?"

"Yes, Daddy. I'll be good." The little boy hung his head, avoiding Daddy's eyes.

"If you drop your crayons today, you are not to crawl underneath the pews to get them until after the service."

"Okay. But Daddy, when my red crayon got dropped on the floor, I couldn't finishing coloring my fire truck. Fire trucks are red."

"I know they are, but when you put your hand on Mrs. Mathson's leg and she screamed, the whole service stopped. It wasn't nice to scare that poor woman that way!" Daddy was maintaining his serious composure with effort.

"Old Mrs. Mathson was stepping on my crayon, and I was just trying to . . ."

". . . move her foot," finished Dad. "I know, son. I know. Mrs. Mathson didn't know that, but to have a hand grab her leg that way during the sermon was a bit of a surprise."

"She didn't need to jump up and scream 'Oh Lordy' that way. I didn't do that part," Bob defended.

"We've been all through this before. You are not, under any circumstances—"

"And old Mr. Mathson yelled 'amen,' and I didn't even touch him." Bob was waging war on injustice now.

Daddy was having trouble continuing his lecture as he remembered the scene from the previous Sunday. It had been memorable. Staring with renewed sternness at the five-year-old in front of him, Dad knelt down to be at eye level.

"Now listen to me. Today you will not crawl under the seats, no matter what crayon you lose. Also, you are never again to attempt to push a lady's leg around, and you are not to scream out—"

"But she stepped on my hand when she stood up Daddy. That hurt—"

"Now listen! You are to stay in the pew once we are seated and not move until the service is over. Furthermore, when we get home today, you are to repeat to me exactly what the preacher said. Is that clear?"

"Everything?" Bob asked in wide-eyed disbelief.

"Everything!"

"Every single word?"

"Every word of the sermon." Daddy was serious now. "If you can't behave today, I will have to be stern with you when we get home." It was a proclamation, and Bob knew it.

"You would spank me?" he asked.

"I wouldn't want to spank you, but if you don't stay in your seat and color quietly, I will have to do just that. The test will come when we get home."

"When I tell you the sermon?"

"When you tell us the sermon. Neither you nor anyone else could have remembered last Sunday's sermon, son. By the time you finished getting your red crayon back, the whole service was a shambles. Our pastor was most upset, and your poor old Daddy had the face-ache." With all his heart Daddy loved the little boy staring back at him, but he was not about to repeat the scene of the previous Sunday. His patience only extended so far, but it was often too far for Mother.

"Bob," Mother added, "Daddy means every word he is saying. And when Daddy gets finished, I just may add a couple of licks of my own to that spanking he is going to give you!" She had been embarrassed by his behavior the previous week.

"Now, Grace. If Bob hears all of the sermon, he won't have time to recreate the chaos of last week. Will you, son?"

"No, sir. I'll be good. I promise."

"That's good. You will be a good boy. You can count on that, Mother," Daddy reassured her. Daddy believed in discipline. Likewise, he believed that love created more confidence and that good expectations paid greater dividends than all the spankings in the world.

As we left for church, Bob kept pulling at the back of his pants. After every few steps he would stop and yank determinedly as if to give his Sunday britches greater length.

"Honey, are your pants too little again?" Mother asked. She looked anxiously at Bob's clothing like a seamstress about to do a fitting. "I do believe they are too short already! We just bought that pair last month!"

"Yeah, but it's not the short that's bothering me. These pants come up too high in the between crack."

"They certainly do, and they are almost too little around, too. Do the best you can today, and we will buy you another pair before next Sunday," she assured him.

The service had already begun when we arrived. The congregation was standing, singing, as we entered. An usher who met us led us down the aisle to an empty pew three rows from the front. We were directly in front of the pulpit. Old Spice aftershave mixed uncomfortably with the too-sweet scent of Evening in Paris perfume; and they blended into the lighter fragrance of the large bouquet of fresh flowers on the altar table. It was difficult to breathe in the already too-hot sanctuary. The well-dressed women around us were wearing their Sunday best, complete with tiny hats on their professionally finger-waved hairdos. The stage was set for a formal Sunday service, as usual.

As we took our places in the pew, I noticed with relief that only two couples were seated in the row in front of us. Daddy sat next to the aisle, next to Bob. I sat on the other side of Bob, and Mother sat next to me. Bob quickly took up his coloring book pose, two people wide and in a reclining position. He was eager to prove to Daddy that today was going to be different.

As the song ended, the congregation was seated. Bob began leafing through his coloring book determined to stay busy and out of trouble. But his efforts were too great. He slapped one page onto the next, noisily popping the heavy paper. Daddy looked straight ahead. As Bob reached the last page, he sighed heavily and handed me the book.

"What's the matter?" I whispered.

"No more spacemen and no more rockets. Nothing but bunny rabbits and kitty cats left," he answered in a louder-than-a-stage-whisper voice.

Dad shot Bob a warning glance. I whispered softly, my mouth close to Bob's ear, "You had better color if you know what's good for you."

People in the pews behind us shuffled, searching for comfortable positions. The ceiling fans overhead stirred the hot, humid morning air. Nearly everyone was making a gallant effort to operate one of the cardboard hand fans with the picture of Jesus printed on one side. These were compliments of the local funeral parlor. The prickly summer heat seemed to stand still in spite of all the manual effort.

The little boy at my side stirred and rearranged himself on the seat beside me. Sighing in resignation, he searched anew for an interesting picture to color. I turned to give my attention to the service.

The pastor was reading his text from the Bible. "And the Lord commanded—"

"Give me my crayon box!"

The voice beside me pierced the air. I froze, then glanced at Daddy. He could have been a statue carved in stone as he stared straight ahead. Bob stretched on the seat with his open coloring book. He had found the elusive box, but he was well aware of what he had done. He had forgotten—again. He held the wayward box in a death grip, his eyes tightly shut. It was a long time before I breathed again. By the time I did, Bob was coloring with great determination a large bunny rabbit on the page in front of him.

The heat was stifling. Bob shifted his position. As he did, the crayon box hit the floor, and crayons rolled in all directions. Bob lay very still. Daddy continued to stare at the preacher while I waited several moments to regain my normal breathing.

Bob gradually sat upright, all the while looking intensely at the preacher. I watched in disbelief as Bob, with slow, almost imperceptible movement slipped off one shoe with the help of his other foot. Slowly, deliberately, he slid slightly forward, gingerly wrapping his stocking toes around the first crayon within his grasp. Gradually he pulled the crayon backward until it was within reaching distance, then quietly leaned forward and picked it up. Then he began a second rescue mission, raking in the next crayon. After he retrieved it, he began a third trip, but Daddy was aware of the operation. With the slightest shake of his head, Dad indicated the crayon mission was finished.

Bob sat dejectedly for a moment, then began coloring the bunny bright purple. Any color was fine with me as long as he stayed still.

The heat was smothering now. The hand fans only stirred the scorching air while the ceiling fans worked determinedly overhead. But nothing helped.

Suddenly the purple crayon was airborne as Bob twitched in his seat, digging at his legs with both hands.

"I itch!" he shouted as he pulled at his trousers. Daddy glared at Bob, but the little boy was obviously miserable.

The pastor's voice interrupted ". . . and now go into all the world and—"

"Itch!" shouted Bob. He had out-shouted the preacher, and he had no intention of stopping. The heat and the partly wool pants had joined forces now.

"Jesus said—"

"Scratch! I've got to scratch," wept the little fellow as he continued to pull frantically at the offending trousers.

Daddy and I both tried to help him find a more comfortable position, but without success. The pants and the heat were winning the battle.

"Pray the Lord will—"

"Scratch my behindermost parts!" Bob wiggled frantically in the seat.

"Amen."

The little fellow had lost control. He was obviously miserable now. The pastor was pale as he glanced in Bob's direction, but Daddy was already leading Bob up the aisle. We were the first family out the door that day. Bob frantically pulled off his pants on the front steps and left them there for me to pick up as he raced to the car in his underwear.

Once safely at home, we gathered in the living room as Bob carefully prepared to deliver his morning sermon. In the comfort of his cotton overalls and no shirt, his bare toes wiggling on the cool floor, he stood solemnly behind an end table he had arranged as his pulpit. Opening his little Bible, he read his version of the Bible verses, from memory of course. "Let the little children come to me," he announced, and then he gave a replay of what the sermon had meant to him. It did have some references to kitty cats and bunny rabbits, but they were all "God's little children," too. His sermon was sincerely touching, and we listened in disbelief. He had heard a lot considering all that had happened. When he had finished, Daddy put his arms around his son.

"You had a very fine sermon, honey. A very fine sermon."

"I'm sorry I was bad, but I itched," Bob said.

Daddy shook his head. "If I had heard half of all you heard after everything that happened in church today, I'd be a much better man than I am. A much better man."

Daddy sat there a long time, his arms around his little boy.

A Childhood Home

I LIVED IN THE UGLIEST PLACE IN TOWN. It wasn't even a house, just two atticlike rooms on top of my parents' café. It was rumored that the whole place had once been an ice plant. I never could figure that one out since we already had a rather ancient ice plant at the end of Main Street, but whatever it had been, it was never intended to be someone's home.

Those two rooms were set to the back of the brick building that was the café, but this second story was also built of brick. The two doors, one from each room, opened onto a boardwalk leading down a rickety outside stairway off the alley. The toilet was an afterthought, placed in front of the two rooms but outside like an outdoor privy, circa 1900, except that it did have running water.

Inside, Mother and Dad had done what they could to make the makeshift warehouse rooms into a home. But what can be done with eighteen-foot ceilings and twelve-foot windows? Very little that will make them warm and cozy. However, for ten of my most formative years, that was the place I called "home."

Living there, being embarrassed by those worse than ugly surroundings, made me determined someday to own a pretty home. So it was with complete disbelief that I listened as Jeanne, a friend of mine, asked to move in with us. Jeanne's mother, Elvina, along with Jeanne, often worked in the café on busy days. On especially busy days, her father, Wade, had also been coaxed into action.

The idea made sense. Jeanne's parents lived a few miles out into the country. There she had to ride the school bus. If she lived with us, she could walk to school and be in more extracurricular activities. And she would have more time to work in the café for extra money.

An agreement was reached, and Jeanne moved in, making five of us sharing that limited space: Daddy, Mother, me, Jeanne, and my little brother, Bob, who must have been four or five at that time.

Instead of this arrangement being overcrowded, Jeanne's coming just added to the fun. After all, Dad and Mother opened the café by five-thirty each morning and seldom got back up to bed until ten-thirty or eleven at night. So once we kids were upstairs, we had the place to ourselves. That much freedom presented a variety of options for having a good time.

One of our favorite games was playing Frankenstein. Naturally, I played Frankenstein. I was duly inspired when playing this role.

At night, we turned out the lights and opened up the doors and windows. This game only took place in the summer because the doors and windows had to be open to give the proper effect. With the streetlights streaming through the openings, I'd go outside and make my entrance. With my legs and arms stiff, my head held high, nearly goose-stepping as I entered the doorway, my shadow on the walls was enough to scare even me. Both Jeanne and Bob would jump in the middle of the bed and, clutching each other, would scream and cry to the top of their lungs. Although no one was on the streets below by this time of night, it wasn't a good idea to get Dad and Mother's unfavorable attention after a long day. Also, there was the outside chance that the sheriff might be making some nightly rounds below.

Once I stopped the game out of common sense and self-preservation, Bob and Jeanne would begin begging me to be Frankenstein "just one more time," and they wouldn't scream this time. But it never worked out that way. Each time they seemed to scream louder than before.

We played numerous games up there, such as spitting on passersby down below during the day and joyfully, but silently, counting the number of direct hits.

On some nights when we went upstairs, we would turn out the lights and read Nancy Drew books by flashlight. The shadows on the wall and the many imaginary noises were enough to scare any normal adult. That explained why I found Bob asleep in his little wicker rocker one night in the drop-dead heat of an Oklahoma summer. He had a Nancy Drew book open on his lap, but perspiration was streaming down his face because he had on his heavy winter jacket, gloves, and cap with the earmuffs pulled down! So much for the imagination.

The one incident that far outdistanced our Frankenstein games and Nancy Drew stories had nothing to do with either. Instead, it was a practical joke I played on Jeanne.

Each morning we dressed Bob and sent him downstairs for breakfast, then got ready for school ourselves. High school girls have always taken longer to get ready than the majority of the human race. Girls call it attention to detail; it seems like vanity from any other point of view.

It was cold that morning. As usual, Jeanne was wearing her bra and panties and was in the midst of applying her makeup when she had to go to the bathroom. Once she was outside, I locked all the doors and windows and waited. It was daylight, and with less than an hour before school, the sidewalks were filled with school kids and the street with its morning traffic.

Jeanne discovered she had been exiled when she rushed back to open the door. I was deaf to her pleading. For fifteen minutes, Jeanne hid in the toilet, or behind it, until the streets below were deserted, then rushed to the door and frantically flung her scantily clad body at the bolted opening. She pleaded, threatened, and cried.

I was enjoying her misery. Spotting a man across the street on the sidewalk below, I yelled to him, calling attention to Jeanne's dilemma. He stopped and stared, then made his way toward the café. I was dead and I knew it. Mother and Dad would kill me. So I opened the door, and Jeanne fell through it, shivering from cold and embarrassment and threatening violence even the Geneva Convention restrains. I was almost sorry. She had suffered—no doubt about it—but being kids we laughed and cried at our own foolishness.

Jeanne and I are still friends today. When we talk by phone, one of us always mentions the day she got locked outside in the cold, and we laugh while sharing those moments from long ago.

When I think of that ugly place I called home during those years, it still brings a shiver. A lot of love was shared there, making what Daddy said almost true: "It isn't the buildings that matter but the people inside."

THE TORNADO

THE DEEP GUTTERAL GROAN BEGAN IN the depths of the town's breast. It gathered speed and intensity as it began its relentless climb up the tonal scale. Graduating to a mighty shriek, the tornado alarm could be heard for miles—sustained, relentless, unforgiving. With the alarm box less than a small city block away, it might as well have been directly underneath our pillows.

Once the siren crested, it hung at its highest note for what seemed to be several minutes. Then, beginning its downward skid into the deep menacing groans of its beginning, it fell as suddenly as it had risen. This was the same alarm, the same sound that signaled fires. The difference was how long the topmost screech hung in mid-air. The alarm's high, sustained scream struck fear into the hearts of everyone, even adults.

Tornado warnings seldom caught us entirely by surprise. In the spring during the heaviest of the tornado seasons, the "makings of a cloud" often lay along the southwestern horizon late in the afternoon. It gradually gathered strength as small, innocent-looking, low-lying clouds gently puffed into huge white, marshmallowy mounds, then turned dark and menacing by late evening. As night fell, playful streaks of lightning darted and chased each other. This freelance electrical game of cat and mouse grew bolder until the western sky was a shadowy flashing of light and dark.

On such nights, the air was usually hot, sultry, and almost breathless. As we sat under what the weatherman called a "disappearing high," it was chased by an "incoming low" as the cold air from the Rocky Mountains met the warm, humid air from the Gulf of Mexico.

Old-timers called the rains that could accompany such dramatic meetings "frog stranglers," but these springtime rainstorms could strangle more than frogs when conditions spawned a series of twisters, which happened often. On evenings like this, sturdy shoes, jeans, shirts, and other quick-dress specials were left in handy, organized piles. With the beginning of that low throaty growl, dressing became quick business, and if the storm was too close, these dressing rituals could become marathons to be accomplished in flight. These tricky sleight-of-hand races against time had some humorous outcomes. Even the most carefully stacked necessities could become unstacked as each of us searched frantically for our clothing.

"'That's it! I told you we would have a storm," cried Jeanne, flying out of bed.

"Get up, Bob. We've gotta get you dressed, guy. Your mother thinks little boys should wear more than underwear and pajamas to the cellar. I'm in favor of getting there first myself. What good is my body, dressed or undressed, if it's dead?"

Jeanne babbled in her fright as she quickly grabbed for clothes. She dressed herself and helped me dress four-year-old Bob at the same time.

"Bob, where are your overalls?" I cried impatiently. "And get your shirt on right side around. You can't button it down the back! Jeanne, you have on one of my shoes and one of yours. Give me my shoe!" I demanded, shaking in fright.

"What shoe? Grab two and go! We'll trade later. We wear the same size. A shoe is a shoe, I always say. If it fits, wear it to the cellar, then give it back!"

"But I can't find your other shoe, and the one on your right foot is mine!"

"Tough! I'm getting your brother dressed. Just reach under that bed and get another shoe. I had 'em both there when we started. It's there. Look for it. Bobs, where are your shoes? Bobs, wake up and help look for your stupid shoes, for heaven's sake!"

The wind was off the cloud now, and the rush and roar of the gusts let us know the storm meant business. While our dressing trials intensified as we lost and found our things, a drama of a different kind was taking place in Mother and Dad's bedroom. By the time the storm siren had finished its eerie screaming, Daddy had turned on the radio. Because of the accompanying electrical storm, the static was the loudest part of the broadcast. However, he was usually able to catch just enough of the details to relay the information. Getting dressed was not the biggest of their problems. They had left the café not long after the warning was sounded, but Mother always had to have on "Sunday makeup" and her hair carefully arranged before she could enter anyone's cellar.

"Grace," Dad began, "there is a tornado funnel on the ground fifteen miles southwest of town. We need to leave now!"

"Jeff, does my hair look all right in the back?" she questioned, holding a hand mirror up to the larger one for a better view. She was forever checking her hair because of a bald spot in back.

"Yes, honey. Don't worry about your hair. That funnel is

a bad one and moving fast. It is still on the ground heading directly toward town. It is ten miles out now."

"I just want my hair to cover my head in the back—you know. Help me out here," she pleaded, searching for better light in the mirror.

"For goodness sakes Grace, that funnel is still on the ground five miles out. We've got to get out of here!" By this time Dad had passed the point of patience. "I'll see if the children are ready to go. You must stop all this 'Sunday-go-to-meetin' getting ready. We must go, Grace!"

"Children," Daddy called "are you ready to go?"

Ready or not, our answers were always in the affirmative. "Bob's ready and we are, almost. But we can't find the cat. He's hiding someplace," I called back. Snoopy always got scared when the siren went off, but we always took him with us. Once he was cradled in someone's arms, he was okay. He had been to the cellar as often as we had—nothing would have persuaded us to leave him.

Daddy had lighted a lantern, and as we raced down the rickety outside stairway, Mother was carefully checking that her hair was still under her scarf! The wind was howling, beating our clothing around our legs. Thoroughly windblown, we reached the alley, and turned into the wind. The cellar was now a little more than a block away, but it seemed much farther with the constant flashing of lightning! The wind caught the fans of the windmills stored on the vacant lot off the alley, spinning them crazily in the flashing light and giving them the appearance of skeletons bearing down on us. We kids were certain they were going to catch us!

"Bob, where are your shoes?" Jeanne suddenly yelled.

"I lost 'em," Bob screamed, stopping to stare behind him.

"Here's one shoe," I shouted, above the wind.

"Norene, you grab one hand. I'll grab the other, and let's just carry him. The gravel will kill his feet, and the storm is on us."

"But I've got the cat," I yelled.

"Grab him with your other hand. He isn't that heavy."

So with the wind blowing dirt and debris in our faces, we raced on, Snoopy on my shoulder, each of us holding Bob by a hand and lifting him above the alleyway as we ran. Occasionally, we let him hit the ground for a step or two, and he'd scream, "You pull too fast!"

Dad and Mother were behind us with the lantern, wearing raincoats. Mother, as always, was in her scarf.

Once we arrived at the cellar, Jeanne stomped on the slanting door leading down to the haven below us. Safety was only five steps down now. The noise brought action as the door was raised for us to enter.

"It's Jeff's family," someone shouted from deep inside. We clambered down the steps just as the first big drops of rain splashed above us.

The cellar was full of townsfolk. We were the last to arrive. It was easy to see why. We were the only fully dressed people there. Women in curlers and housecoats hastily pulled on over nightgowns and men with overalls and no shirts stood around the underground cement-walled room. Several lanterns cast a yellow glow that turned to shadowy shapes on the walls.

"Why, Grace, you look nigh on ready for church," laughed one of the women. "And here I have my hair in curlers and not even a hair net!"

"Boy, where's your shoes?" someone asked as Daddy lifted Bob to his shoulders.

"I lost 'em comin'," he answered, and everybody laughed.

"Y'all heard about the old farmer who kept comin' outta the cellar disappointed becuz' things was always just as he left 'em, and he figured he'd come down fur nothin'. Always just made him mad somehow. Finally, he lifted the cellar door after the wind quit, and thar warn't nuthin' fur as far as he could see in any direction. Everything was wiped cleaner than a whistle. He rared back and said, 'Now, that's the way I like to see it!'"

Everyone laughed as the storm roared above us, rain and wind gusting in mighty sheets. "I'd just as soon stay disappointed at what the storm didn't do," someone commented.

"Me too, yeah, me too," heads nodded agreement in the lantern light.

Gradually the rain slowed and the roar calmed as the thunder moved on. We gathered our personal things and mounted the steps leading back to the world outside where the rain continued steady and subdued.

The trek home contrasted sharply to the frantic trip of a few minutes earlier. The windmill fans were now slick, shiny metal panels glimmering in the light of our lantern, instead of ghostly skeletons.

Daddy carried Bob while Jeanne took Mother's arm. Snoopy settled himself on my shoulder for the ride home.

"Things are blown around a little, but otherwise everything looks fine," Dad said in approval.

"Yeah, every time we make this run, I just know we won't make it," commented Jeanne. "Especially since we are always the best-dressed family there."

As we reached home, we were all laughing.

"Yep, and Mother always has the prettiest hairdo around," I joked. "But it never gets that way until the funnel is on the ground five miles out of town!"

SPACE FLIGHT

"JEFF, IS YOUR SON HERE?" CLEMENT asked.

"No, I guess he isn't," Dad answered, "but I saw him only a few minutes ago back there in his rocking chair. He was asleep." Dad looked surprised.

The garage owner from across the street had asked the question. He stood now in the doorway of the café, appearing both concerned and confused.

"Is there a problem?" asked Dad.

"Probably not, Jeff. I just thought I saw Bob, that's all." Clement's voice trailed off at the end of the sentence, and again he looked worried.

"Clement, you have known that boy since he was a baby. You know whether you saw him or not. You seem worried," Dad prodded.

"I saw a boy about Bob's size, you know, big for a five-year-old. He had on striped overalls and a shirt like Bob wears. He was riding a bicycle."

Both men looked through the front window where Bob's bike was usually parked. It was gone.

"What concerns me is this kid was riding right down the middle of Main Street. That is dangerous enough, but this kid had an ice cream carton over his head."

With the original inquiry about Bob, Mother had come from the kitchen. With the words "carton over his head,"

102

Dad had started untying his apron and walking around the counter toward the door.

"Jeff, that's Bob all right," Mother blustered, her black eyes snapping. "I tried to get you to do something when he started playing spaceman with those dish towels tied around his neck. Jumping off these stools onto that concrete floor was dangerous enough." Her concern for his welfare surfaced in her accusations. Bob had almost died at birth, and Mother feared that something terrible would happen to him. She had lost her first baby, and she was afraid that she would lose one of us.

"I know, Grace. I should have punished him. But he has no real place to play—a yard, like other kids—and it seemed innocent enough at the time."

"Yes, Jeff. Jumping off the stools wasn't really too bad. But last week when someone across the street reported his spaceman act taking place on top of the building, that was dangerous. With that dish towel popping in the wind that way, that child thinks he can fly. I know he does. And I still think he might have jumped. He has too vivid an imagination."

Mother was angry. She felt Dad's discipline was too lax with both Bob and me.

Dad tossed his apron on the counter. "I'll see if it is him."

Several men at the counter put down their coffee cups as if to join the search.

"Keep your seats, fellas," Dad advised. "No reason to get excited. This is just one more of those times a father earns the right to gray hair. I'd hate for Bob to stop traffic. I doubt he is in much danger though."

Less than five minutes later, Daddy was back with Bob in tow, carrying the ice cream carton on his arm like an astronaut might carry his helmet. Dad was calm as he talked with him.

"Now son, it is embarrassing to find people afraid to drive down Main Street for fear of hitting a spaceman in full flight. How did you feel when people had to pull over and stop?"

"I'm sorry, Daddy. I didn't mean to cause a problem," the little fellow apologized contritely.

"I wasn't on Main Street though."

"You weren't? Then where were you?" asked Dad.

"On the moon," explained Bob innocently. "And cars don't go up there."

Dad sat down slowly, realizing the vividness of his son's imagination.

Meanwhile, in the kitchen Bob's most ardent adult fan was intensely involved in the little drama.

"Poor little feller. What are they a-doin' to him now anyways?" fumed Elvina. "He ain't a-hurtin' nobody or doin' nothin' bad."

Elvina, and at times her whole family, worked with us on busy days. Although we were good friends, Bob was clearly her favorite.

"Not many kids can go all the way to the moon with nothing but a cardboard box on their head," she declared.

"Now son," continued Dad, "I'm sure men will walk on the moon in your lifetime. But no doubt their helmets will be equipped with eyeholes so they can see where they are going."

"I had an eyehole, Daddy," Bob answered, pointing to an oval glass securely taped over a small opening on one side of the carton. Dad looked at the small piece of glass and back at Bob. "That explains the disappearance of the crystal from the face of my alarm clock." Bob nodded in agreement, and Daddy grinned in spite of himself.

"I'm sorry if I caused a problem, Daddy," Bob said quietly, then sat down in his little wicker rocker.

Dad thanked Clement for his help. Turning back to Bob,

he noticed the little fellow rocking, slowly at first. Then the rocker gradually moved faster. The little chair tipped forward and backward, continually picking up speed.

From the look on Bob's face, it was clearly evident he was airborne again!

MOTHER AND
WHITE FEATHER

"MAY I HELP YOU?" DAD ASKED QUIETLY
as he placed a glass of water on the counter in front of the
old Indian man hunched forward on the café stool. A black
ten-gallon hat sat squarely on his head, allowing his two
long braids to lie on either shoulder. His face was angry,
and his voice a growl as he muttered, "No speak English."

"Food. Do you want food?" inquired Dad patiently.

"Food!" was the answer. His stance and expression
never changed.

"What kind of food?" Dad questioned.

"Food," the old Indian growled.

Dad looked frustrated. He was getting nowhere.

"Eat?" Dad asked as if to coax any other known English
words from the hunched, frowning figure.

"Yah, eat food!" was the return growl.

Dad was beginning to unravel. The large, formidable
figure in front of him was beginning to tax his almost
unending patience.

"What kind of food? Hamburger?" encouraged Dad,
leaning forward.

The old Indian glowered at Dad from under his hat,
slammed his fist onto the counter, and roared, "Soap and
gravy!"

Dad was nonplussed, but he bravely tried once more.

"Soup and gravy?"

"*Soap* and gravy," roared the return.

Dad had lost it now. Sometimes when he was very tired, the Kiowa Indians tried his patience. Almost all of them spoke English, but frequently they refused to do so. This one was obviously on such a spree, something that often happened when they had been drinking.

"Once more. What do you want to eat?" asked Dad.

"Where your woman? She know soap and gravy," the Indian growled.

That was all the encouragement Daddy needed. Mother could handle these people. She had grown up with them, gone to school with many of them, and had played with them as children.

Dad summoned Mother from the kitchen. "Grace, this man says he wants soap and gravy. I can't understand him."

Mother leaned forward, glancing at Dad as if to show him how to handle the situation. Then she slammed her hand onto the counter and demanded his order.

"Soap and gravy? We have that," she said, rushing back into the kitchen. She was back almost instantly bearing a small plate containing a bar of Procter & Gamble soap covered with gravy. She set it down in front of the large, angry-looking Indian man.

"Soap and gravy! Our specialty!" Mother announced triumphantly, looking directly into the Indian's face. He glared back at her. They stared angrily at each other in silence. It was a standoff. Neither one moved for several seconds.

Then the Indian removed his hat as he continued to stare at Mother. They both burst into laughter.

"A good joke?" he roared. "Grace, you are still as ornery as you were when you were little. Do you remember White Feather?"

Mother stared in disbelief. Then they wrapped their arms around each other, laughing and hugging.

"You grew up and got mean," Mother laughed.

"Ah, Grace, you were always mean. You just grew up!" White Feather laughed.

Dad was laughing and wiping his eyes. Mother seldom had anyone play a joke on her. She and White Feather had gone to school together, and Mother had teased him unmercifully as a child. He had finally evened an old score!

DENNIS

SOUTHWESTERN OKLAHOMA IS INDIAN country, deeded to them by the United States and paid for again over the infamous "Trail of Tears." However, if it had not been for my mother and father, I could have grown up missing the richness of this heritage.

My parents had many Indian friends made when they attended school together in the one-room school days. These friends often came into my parents' little café to eat and exchange memories.

Not until years later did it occur to me that the children of Mom and Dad's Indian friends were not necessarily my friends. Although we attended school together, they played on one side of the playground, and my white friends and I played on the other.

They were distantly friendly when they came to the café for a "humburger and red sodi-pop," but otherwise we hardly knew each other's names.

There were few Indian kids in our music groups in high school, none that I can remember in our school plays or drama competitions. Some played basketball, and played well, but I can't recall many who were singled out for honors. They lived in one world, and we lived in another.

The Indians I knew were "just people." They kept to themselves, seldom showing their feelings publicly. Usually their faces were masks, and what went on behind them rarely showed.

However, one exception will remain vividly imprinted in my memory. Dennis's grandmother was different from every Indian I ever knew.

Today this lady probably would be fined or jailed for child abuse. Then her performance was a show to watch in disbelief.

When Dennis and his grandmother came into the café, Jeanne, her mother Elvina, my brother Bob, and I often drew straws to see which one of us got the short straw and, thus, the chance to take their orders. There we could watch again the same volley of emotions unleashed. Though it happened numerous times, the dialogue was almost always the same.

A half-breed Indian/white boy, Dennis evidently had been pawned off on his Indian grandmother who, according to all appearances, hated him. They would make their entrance with Grandmother shoving Dennis ahead of her by a foot or two with each succeeding shove.

"Sit down, Den-nuss," she would shout, roughly pushing him into a booth. Pulling her brightly colored shawl closer around her shoulders, she would sit down opposite him.

Glaring angrily into his dirty little face, she would demand, "What do you want, Den-nuss?" There would be no reply, and the question would be stated a second time, a bit louder.

"I say, Den-nuss, what you want?" Still no answer.

Enraged by the stiff, dirty, partly white face in front of her, the grandmother would gradually lose control. Grabbing the little baseball cap Dennis always wore, she would beat him in the face and on the head and ears, accompanied by a hint of why they had come in the first place.

"Den-nuss, you want humburger?" she would shout, stopping the beating only long enough for him to nod his head. Then she would resume the activity with even greater vigor.

"Then tell the lady you want humburger!" she shouted, sometimes getting in a lick or two midsentence.

Round two would begin when the question of a drink was mentioned. Richly inspired by her former successful communication, she would snatch the well-worn cap from Dennis's head and repeat the ritual, but with renewed enthusiasm.

"You want sodi-pop?" she would shout at full volume, whipping the cap back and forth across Dennis's head. Again there would be no reaction.

Standing up for better aim at her target, she would address the question again.

"You want red sodi-pop?" she shouted louder. Finally, the bowed head would nod an affirmative answer. That would be her cue for the final crescendo. "Then tell the lady you want red sodi-pop!" By then she was screaming, beating on Dennis all the while.

I don't think Dennis ever spoke a word. He might have muttered "sodi-pop." If so, his lips barely moved.

Once the order was taken, the show was usually over until their next visit. The hamburger and red soda pop were consumed in silence. There was never a crumb left on Dennis's plate or a drop of red in the bottom of the bottle. Either he was very hungry, or he had similar encouragement at home to clean his plate, possibly both.

Early one morning I observed a variation on the ritual enacted beside the corner drugstore that also served as a Greyhound bus station. Grandma obviously had been planning a trip to Anadarko, the Indian capital of Oklahoma, to see the Indian agent there. However, all had not gone as planned, and Dennis and his grandmother had missed the bus.

Again the baseball cap was the weapon as Grandma angrily beat Dennis on the head and in her frustration kept shouting, "Stop that bus, Den-nuss. Get down to the next corner. Tell bus driver your grandma has to go to Ana-Darko."

Dennis attempted to do as he was told, trying to outrun the bus as it circled the block to leave town, but he was too late. The bus passed within a few feet of him, but he was small for his eleven or twelve years, and the driver did not see his frantic waving.

By this time Grandma had caught up with him, shawl and all, ball cap still in hand.

"Why you not stop that bus, Den-nuss? You stupid kid. You make your grandma late, and now we can't go Ana-Darko," she yelled between slaps with the cap.

Her performances must have been intended for a white audience because she spoke to Dennis in English. I had seen her in the company of other Kiowa women, and she carried on her conversation with them in the Kiowa language. Her angry outbursts at her grandson, however, were in the language the white man could understand. Maybe she only spoke English to Dennis, further excluding him from his own race. I don't know.

Years passed. There were no reports in the newspapers of a young Indian man killing his grandmother, but it wouldn't have surprised me. The sad possibility is that Dennis may have grown up, beatings and all, to become another Indian statistic as he turned to drugs or alcohol to fill the loneliness in his heart where love should have lived.

Screen Door Customers

"MISSAH MURPHEY, CAN WE COMES IN? We is hungry and we ain't gots no other place that lets us eat."

The face peering through the kitchen screen door was black. The question was polite, even pleading.

"Jeff," barked Mother in her lowest angry voice, "they are back. It is your fault, so you can take care of them."

Daddy was the only café owner around who fed black workers. No blacks lived in or around town that I recall, and they only appeared during cotton-picking time.

"You are always welcome anytime you want to eat, fellas," Dad answered, smiling as he unlatched the kitchen screen. "Just give me a minute to clean off the work table, and we will get you some knives, forks, and napkins and some water to drink."

"Norene," Dad called, "forget the cash register for a minute. I need a setup back here for three." Daddy spoke just loud enough to be heard. He never said anything about being willing to feed blacks, but some of his regular customers knew and didn't like it. They even mentioned it occasionally, but Daddy had a quick but firm answer. No one brought it up with him more than once. "Only God knows why he didn't see fit to make me a black man instead of a white one," he would say quietly. "But, you

113

know, I doubt a man's race will make much difference when we get to heaven." Daddy meant what he said, and because the townsfolk respected him, they never argued.

Mother did! She had no prejudice toward the Kiowa Indians who ate with us. She knew many of them from her school days. But the red man and the black man occupied separate places in her mind. She didn't understand the black men and was afraid that our white customers wouldn't come back.

"Now Jeff, we took the Indian's land. They were here first," she would argue, "but the blacks came as slaves, and they should stay slaves or we should just send them back!" Her eyes would snap black fire when she said it.

As I took the necessary utensils to the kitchen, I kept my distance from Mother. During such times she banged more pots, clattered, and occasionally shattered, more dishes while muttering under her breath to show her disapproval.

The black men who sometimes came to the kitchen door had heard from others in the fields that black people could be served at the screen door entrance. They were always appreciative, and yet so subservient. Their gazes never met ours because their heads were down. They were painfully aware of their less-than-equal place in society in the forties.

Daddy always carried on a conversation with any of the men who would talk. They discussed the crops and almost always the weather. Each time Daddy welcomed them into the kitchen, it was with the same apology, "Fellas, I'm sorry I can't offer you better seats, but we will do all we can to make you comfortable. You are welcome to everything we have on the menu. I would be happy to have you up front like everyone else, but our white customers just don't see it that way."

Mother would mumble a bit louder, bang a pot or two,

and shoot Dad a warning glance. When the meal was over, the black men would pay Daddy or me. They were always grateful and polite, and Daddy would follow them out the back door with an ongoing invitation, "Glad to have you gentlemen, and you know you are always welcome to eat here whenever you are in town."

"We thank ya, Missah Murphey. That chicken-fried steak shore hits the spot!"

The conversation between Mother and Daddy was of the cookie-cutter variety—always the same. "Now Jeff, if you keep feeding those men like that, we will lose our regular trade because of it, and you know I'm right." Mother would insist, but Daddy never agreed and never gave in.

When Rosa Parks later refused to give up her seat on that bus in Alabama, Mother was sure Daddy's goodness was going to backfire on him. "Just what will you do, Jeff Murphey, the first time those kitchen customers of yours come through that front door and sit down and order? What then?"

"I don't know, Grace. I just don't know. You are right. Our white customers wouldn't like it. But when a man's hungry, he is hungry. Hunger has no color. Let us pray that Alabama is a long way from here in more ways than one."

At that time, it was. I'm glad that barrier wasn't broken while Daddy owned the café. I don't know what he would have done, but I do know what his heart would have told him to do.

NUGENE

"NUGENE IS DIRTY AGAIN, NO'ENE," BOB
explained as I finished rewashing his knees. Every Saturday afternoon Bob and his little friend Nugene went to
the Saturday matinee to watch Roy Rogers, Gene Autry, or
Hopalong Cassidy. It was a weekend ritual all the young-
sters of the community enjoyed and anticipated.

"Didn't his ear stay pinned to the clothesline like he
promised?" I asked seriously.

"Nope. Musta forgot," Bob replied.

Since it wasn't possible to clean up one little boy and
keep him clean while I washed the other, we had a game.
I "pinned" an ear of one of them to the clothesline on
the rooftop in front of our two-room apartment while I
washed the other. The "ear to the clothesline" was only
in our imaginations, but it was a game they loved to
play. Usually the "clean kid" stayed with his ear on the
clothesline until the other was clean enough to accompany him. But today Nugene had forgotten.

The little three-year-old was Bob's favorite friend. He
belonged to Mildred, a young woman who had come to
work for Daddy when she was twenty and she immediately became another member of our family. Bob had
been a baby at the time, and she had carried him around
so much that some people thought he was hers. Once
word of our new waitress got around, several young men
of marriageable age suddenly started eating in the café.

Each time someone asked her for a date, I added him to the growing list. All of these would-be suitors were carefully screened by me and duly commented on. My list had grown rather lengthy by the time John appeared on the scene.

John was shy, older, and obviously interested. I liked him immediately. Mildred had become like an older sister, and I pictured myself as her guardian. I told myself it was my duty to look out for her welfare and best interests. John came in several times before he asked her out, but I kept encouraging both of them.

Once the dating began, all other suitors were actively discouraged. It was a relatively short time before they were married, then a year later Nugene, as four-year-old Bob labeled him, was born. From the day he was born, he was our baby. Bob and I baby-sat him and took him for walks. As soon as he was old enough, Nugene became Bob's constant sidekick. Saturday afternoons always found them together at the movies.

As close as our families had become, it wasn't destined to last. Before long we watched with tear-filled eyes as the little family moved to California.

"The opportunities are greater and the pay a little better in the central valleys of California," John said. So we kissed Mildred and him goodbye and clung to little Eugene a long time when the time came for them to leave.

Letters were exchanged. As time passed, I went away to college, married, and began teaching. One day Mother wordlessly handed me a letter from Mildred. I was home for a visit and as a young teacher, with a new husband, hadn't written to her.

Mildred's letter began normally enough, but it didn't continue in that vein:

Dear Family,

I wish I could say we were fine, but unfortunately, that isn't true. Eugene hasn't been feeling well lately. Finally, we took him to the doctor. He has leukemia. Before he gets worse, we are moving home. He doesn't want to die in California where we aren't close to our family. He wants to come home where he can be close to his grandparents, can go fishing, and be close to you. You have always been like our family, too, and that is where he wants to be when he dies—home.

Love,

Mildred, John, "Nugene," and Johnetta

The young family came back. Eugene, now fourteen, fished with his grandpa and grandma in the little stream on their farm. Life went on just as it had before they left, but in spite of everything, Eugene continued to get worse. Nothing could be done.

The town wrapped its arms around the family. Love and encouragement flowed.

"How's the Schmidt boy?" was the question on everyone's lips as Eugene continued to lose ground. "If there is anything we can do. . . ." was the frequent offer.

"Here's a ham. We thought you could use it. We just butchered."

"Just killed a beef. Knew you could use a roast or two."

"Me and my wife got such a mess of green beans we can't eat 'em all. You've not time to think of such."

For months during Eugene's last illnesses, food flowed into the house. People cared, and it showed in little daily acts of kindness. Eugene was prayed for in every church in town, but to no avail.

At the funeral, those who had supported the family earlier continued to show their love. Eugene's body was laid to rest in the little graveyard, but all of us still remember him with love.

I will remember him as Bob's favorite little friend who, along with Bob, had to have his ear "pinned to the clothesline" every Saturday—the only way I could get Bob and Nugene ready for the afternoon matinee.

THE TEN-DOLLAR BILL

THE CAFÉ SCREEN DOOR SLAMMED. THE hot, muggy air seemed to stand still, smothering all of us.

"It's already ninety degrees, and it ain't even noon," cried Elvina, putting on her apron. "Today is gonna be another scorcher. I just went to the grocery store and got a little sack of groceries and—wouldn't you know it?—I didn't have any money with me. I left the sack at the cash register for safe keepin' and told 'em I'd be back later. Wade, would you go over un git 'em?" She turned to her husband, who was sitting on one of the stools at the counter drinking his midmorning coffee.

"Oh, it's too hot to move," he answered. "Why don't you get Bob to go. Bob, I'll give you a nickel to run over to the store and pick up Elvina's groceries."

"Canna' go, Mom?" Bob asked as he got up from his wicker rocker.

"How much is your allowance, Bob?" Wade asked.

"A dime," Bob replied, "a dime a week."

"With this heat, I'll raise you a nickel. I'll give you a dime to go get them groceries!" Wade dug in his pocket for another nickel. Handing the money to Bob, he reached for his wallet.

"All I got is a couple of ten-dollar bills. Take this one and bring me the change," Wade instructed.

"Wait a minute, Bob," Mother called, coming from the kitchen. "That is a lot of money. You might lose it. We

120

haven't gone to the bank, and I only have a few ones in the register. Why don't you wait until we get some change for that ten? Jeff will be back with the money from the bank anytime now."

Mother worried about Bob. She knew he often lost things.

"Naw, he'll be careful, won't you, Bob? Just bring me the change. He's a big boy, ain't ya', Bob?" Wade patted Bob on the head and handed him the bill.

It was a busy morning and a hot one. The swamp cooler on top of the café was working overtime, but the day's humidity made its task nearly impossible. Swamp coolers were relatively effective when the humidity was low, but on muggy days they only stirred the scorching air.

Doughnuts were served, most of them accompanied by ice-cold Cokes, but die-hard coffee drinkers drank hot coffee in spite of the temperature.

"Hot coffee makes ya' cooler, I always say. A day ain't a day without ma' coffee," a regular customer sighed as he licked his lips and wiped his sweaty brow.

The coffee and doughnut crowd had come and gone before anyone noticed Bob was still not back. It had been nearly forty-five minutes, and he was nowhere to be seen.

"Grace, have you seen Bob?" Elvina asked. "He sure has been gone a long time. 'Spose he's all right?"

Just then Daddy came through the front door, the money sack from the bank in his hand. Bob trudged along by his side. Both looked worried.

"Bob, are you okay?" worried Elvina. "Was it just too hot for you, honey?"

"No, I'm not hot!" Bob said worriedly, looking at Daddy and back at Elvina. "You must not have given me that ten-dollar bill. When I got to the store, it wasn't in my pocket. I looked all over, and Daddy helped me. I couldn't have lost it." Bob looked sick.

"Bob, you left here with it. What did you do with it?" Mother asked in frustration.

"I didn't have it. I didn't, honest!"

The six-year-old boy stared hard at the floor, blinking back tears.

"Now, you don't cry, Bobs," begged Elvina, kneeling down in front of him and wiping his tears. All of us were her dear friends, but Bob was her favorite.

"Just think with me. You went out the front door and up the street. Where did you cross over to the store? In front of the Ford Garage?"

Bob nodded, still wiping tears.

"Okay. You crossed the street and went into the grocery store. Did you have anything else in your pockets?" she questioned, trying to help him remember.

Bob stopped suddenly and stared at Elvina, wide-eyed. "I know what I did with it!" he squealed, looking relieved.

"You do? See, that was easy wasn't it? Where is it, Bob?"

"I made it into a paper airplane and sailed it. It sailed real good!" Bob said, looking pleased as he remembered the flight.

Mother and Elvina stared at each other and back at the smiling little boy between them. Daddy stopped counting the money for the cash register and stared with fixed concentration at the small stranger smiling up at him. Wade turned on the stool where he was sitting.

"Say that again. I don't think I heard you."

"I sailed it," answered Bob, still unaware of what he was saying.

Dad walked around the counter and knelt beside Bob. "You made a paper airplane out of that ten-dollar bill and sailed it?" Dad asked carefully. "When was the last time you saw it?"

Bob looked at Dad, perplexed. "When it sailed into that car window in front of the Ford Garage." Just as he said "sailed in the car window," his face fell. He stared at the four adults staring at him.

"Oh my. When it became an airplane, it wasn't a ten-dollar bill anymore. It wasn't, honest, it wasn't!" The tears came now because the reality of what he had done had suddenly struck him. The ten-dollar bill and the airplane finally became one.

Dad stood up, went to the cash register, opened it, took out a ten-dollar bill, and handed it to Wade.

Wade shook his head. "You don't owe me anything, Jeff, because this whole thing is my fault. Grace tried to get me to wait until you came with change. I wouldn't do it! Just chalk it up to experience! Bob didn't mean to do it."

"That is it, Bob!" snapped Mother. "You will pay back the money, every penny of it. You will earn it and pay it back!" Mother was angry, and her black eyes snapped as she glared at Bob. "Did you hear me?"

Bob stood still, staring in disbelief. "I will never make ten whole dollars in my whole life," he wailed.

"Oh, yes you will. You will work doing whatever you can and save every penny of it. There will be no more movies on Saturday afternoons, no more ice cream cones . . ." Mother waged her verbal battle on Bob's in-attention.

"Now, Grace. He is just a little feller," begged Elvina. "He didn't meant to do it."

"Now Grace . . ." began Wade. But Mother was having none of it. Someone had to wake this daydreaming child up, and she was going to do it. It was now or never. This was the last straw.

"Stop it, both of you!" commanded Mother. "This time I am in charge of Bob's discipline," she said, glaring at

Dad. "There will be no shortcuts. No easy outs! No fool-ishness. Bob will work and pay back what he has thrown away. Is that clear?"

Mother believed if you loved your child, you would discipline him. She felt honor bound to do it.

By this time Elvina and Wade were almost as upset as Bob. However, they respected Mother's judgment. Still, they hated to see the little fellow punished so severely.

Two weeks passed, then three. Bob hadn't been to the movies, hadn't had any ice cream cones, and had worked at several low-paying odd jobs in the restaurant.

Wade sometimes slipped up beside Bob to ask about his welfare, but each time Mother spotted what she feared might be a breach of the sentence and quickly called Bob away to new duties. She knew Bob had to be taught responsibility. However, late one afternoon Mother and Dad were upstairs resting when Wade came in. Seeing Bob at the counter alone, he sat down beside him.

"How ya' doin', Bob?" asked Wade, ever so gently. "Saved any money?"

"Not much," was the depressed answer.

"How much?"

"'Bout fifty-five cents. I'll be 900 years old when I finally make ten dollars."

"That's really old."

"Yeah, and Roy Rogers and Gene Autry will be dead."

"Yeah. Nine hundred years is a long time."

"Ten dollars is a lot of money."

"Yeah. I've figured out how you can make a dollar right now," Wade whispered.

"A dollar?"

"Shhh—don't tell the world. Your mother will hear."

"How? How?" Bob questioned excitedly.

"You really want to make a dollar?"

"Yeah, you betcha!"

"Okay. Now listen real careful."

"I'll do anything."

"All you have to do is drink a teaspoon of that pepper sauce on the counter there."

"That's all?"

"That's all."

Bob raced around the counter, grabbed a teaspoon, filled it with pepper sauce, and gulped it down. "I did it! That's a dollar!"

Wade stared at Bob in disbelief. "Bob, you better drink some water quick. I didn't think you'd really do that. Here, drink," Wade said, forcing a glass of water to Bob's mouth.

"Where's my dollar?" gurgled Bob.

"Here, right here," cried Wade, quickly reaching for his wallet.

Seeing the dollar, Bob grabbed the pepper sauce bottle and quickly poured another teaspoonful. Before Wade could say more, Bob downed the second teaspoonful.

"Bob, stop that! The game is over. Drink some water. You are going to be sick. Stop it!" pleaded Wade, pushing more water toward Bob.

"That's two dollars!" shouted Bob, reaching for the pepper sauce bottle again.

"No, stop. The game's over!"

A third teaspoonful of the hot liquid streamed into Bob's mouth, followed by more cold water. "Three dollars," screamed Bob, flushed with his sudden wealth.

"Wade Heavener, what are you a doin' to the little feller?" demanded Elvina from the kitchen.

"Tryin' to git 'em to stop! Elvina, git up here!" Wade answered, grabbing the bottle of pepper sauce. But Bob had caught sight of a debt-free life, and nothing was stopping him now. Racing around the counter, he grabbed two full bottles of pepper sauce.

"Stop, Bob, stop!" shouted Elvina, racing in from the kitchen. "Wade, you idiot! What have you done?"

"He is payin' me a dollar for every teaspoon of pepper sauce I drink, and I just lack seven more," squealed Bob, reaching for the spoon again.

"No, no! You take another teaspoon of that fiery stuff, and you will die, Bob. And your mother will kill me for killin' you."

"Here's number four—"

"Bob, stop—I'll pay ya' the other seven dollars fur stoppin'!" shouted Wade.

"I could just kill you, Wade Heavener!" screamed Elvina.

"Here is your ten dollars, Bob. You are out of debt!" screamed Wade, slapping a ten-dollar bill on the counter in front of Bob.

"Mother said I had to earn it, and I'm gonna earn it!" yelped Bob, pulling the top from the pepper sauce bottle. Turning it bottomside up, he began drinking the red hot liquid straight from the bottle.

Elvina grabbed the bottle from him, spilling the red sauce down the front of his shirt and overalls, the counter, and the floor.

"Stop it *now!*" she screeched.

Just then the front door opened, and Mother and Daddy walked in. Seeing the red liquid all over Bob and Elvina and Wade, Mother went into action.

"Jeff, grab a mop. Bob is being sick all over the place!"

"No, I'm not, Mother. Honest. I'm just drinkin' pepper sauce! Wade is paying me—"

"I'm a-payin' 'em to stop," yelled Wade in defense.

"Just what happened here anyway?" asked Dad as he began swabbing up the mess on the floor.

"You wouldn't believe it if I told you!" growled Elvina.

"But when I get this crazy husband of mine home, he may be crippled for life!"

"Lookey, Dad, ten dollars!" squealed Bob.

"Where did you get that?" Mother demanded, her hands on her hips.

"You wouldn't believe it if I told you," groaned Elvina. "Cain't hardly believe it myself!" She glared at Wade.

"Best investment I ever made!" Wade said. "'Specially the last seven dollars of it!"

Then, in spite of the juicy red mess, Bob took the money and handed it back to Wade.

"Here is your ten dollars, Wade!"

"It sure is," Wade smiled, looking pleased. "It sure is." Grabbing Bob's hand and shaking it, he said, "Ten dollars—paid in full!"

THE BASKETBALL GAME

THE GYM DOORS SWUNG OPEN AS THE crowd surged inside. The cold air cut through the aromas of hot dogs and popcorn as people rushed into the warmth and noise of the regional basketball playoffs.

"Get your cushions here—only twenty-five cents apiece. Get one before they are all gone!"

"Concrete slabs make scabs—on your tail," I called. "Rest your tushes on our soft cushions!"

The incoming crowd laughed, and the cushions were soon gone.

"Your mom will kill you if you she hears about what you said."

"I know it, but I rented the rest of the cushions, didn't I?"

The high school gym was almost full as our boys' varsity team played for first place in the regional finals, hoping to make the ultimate goal of state champions. Excitement was running high, and our cushions had sold out.

The seventh-grade Campfire Girls were making money to go to summer camp in the local mountains. Each of our mothers had made several cushions that we rented at every basketball game. Basketball was the highlight of the cold winter months. We always knew that when the wind grew cold, the leaves left the trees, and the snow fell, it was basketball time. Little attention was given to football in our town. Basketball was the school sport. The town came, and we usually won.

This year we had hosted two tournaments, an invitational for all the little towns, ours included, and the regional tournament. This rarely happened. But after a full week of playing, our boys' team had reached the finals. The winner went to state, and community pride was escalating.

By the time the big game started, there were no seats— all the bleachers were full. For a few minutes we had standing room, but it, too, soon disappeared. A few hardy souls shinnied up to the windows on the outside, but the cold wind discouraged all but the most hardy. It was our night, and people from miles around had gathered to cheer our victory against an uptown team from across the state. The competitors had filled almost half the gym, so space was more precious than usual.

Even the popcorn and hot dog sales were difficult because the crowd was so large. Just getting a hot dog and Coke back to the original sittery was nearly impossible, but the concessions soon sold out and nobody cared much since the game was a cliffhanger. By the end of the first half, most of the people had screamed so much their throats hurt. As the second half began, the crowd was on its feet more often than on its seat. One side scored, then the other, and the roar from the gym could be heard all over town if anyone had been out there to hear it. The pressure was on.

Our first string of players had outdone themselves, but our best forward lacked only one more foul and he would be out of the game. We held our breath. Suddenly our opponent had the ball, and the action shifted to the other end of the court. The opposition scored, putting our team two points behind. The other side cheered while we moaned in momentary defeat. Then the ball belonged to us, and the action washed to our end of the court again. Our forward was blocked, and in his frustration he rushed with the ball, unable to throw. Angrily, he threw to another player. Suddenly the whistle blew. Our star forward had fouled out.

Time out. We cheered our star as he walked off the court, then noticed the hurried conference of the coaches. Our next-best player didn't play well under pressure because of his temper, but he was the best to fill the spot. We sensed the delay and read the meaning correctly.

"Number 44, Kenneth Williams for Keith Wright." The coaches had sent Ken in anyway. We held our breath. One and a half minutes remained. We were two points behind, but it was still anybody's ball game. The clocks restarted, and so did the action.

The opposition had the ball, and they were playing "keep away," the old stall. All they had to do was play catch for one and a half minutes, and the championship was theirs. Cheers from their side couldn't override the shouts of "get it, get it" from ours.

Then the action exploded. We stole the ball and took it to our end of the court. "Shoot! Shoot! Shoot!" the crowd chanted as the clock hit one minute, fifty seconds, forty-five seconds. The ball was in the air as the opposition blocked our moves. We moaned, then held our breath. It hit the basket rim, circled it, then lost its momentum and dropped through the hoop! The whole town screamed as the score became tied, with thirty seconds to play.

It was their ball, and the fight was on. But our star guard stole the ball and started back to our end of the court. The crowd went crazy.

In a last-ditch effort to score before the final buzzer, our guard shot the ball to Ken, our stand-in forward. The clock clicked to fifteen seconds, then ten seconds. Without warning, Ken suddenly turned and raced toward the opposition's end of the court. The out-of-towners went crazy as we screamed, "No, no, Ken. No!"

The ball was in the air. It hit the basket and went through the hoop as the final buzzer sounded. Ken had made a basket for the other team.

We had lost the game and the regional because our forward had lost his head. We yelled our disapproval as one of our players landed a hard blow to Ken's jaw and he dropped where he had stood.

The season was really over for us, for our team, and for Ken. The crowd gradually calmed as people reached for wraps and thinned out while making their way toward the exits.

"Gather up the cushions, girls. It's time to count them and go home," our Campfire counselor warned. Still weakened by the excitement of the past few minutes, we gathered and stacked our cushions. It was the last ball game of the year and by far the most exciting.

Unforgettable? Oh, yes, in spite of the outcome. Ken Williams had made history, history we recall even today.

SNOOPY

"MAMA, CAN I KEEP IT? IT FOLLOWED me home," explained six-year-old Bob, tightly clutching the little kitten in his arms.

"Oh honey, not another alley cat. You know what happened to the last one. I thought we agreed," lamented Mother.

"I remember. Somebody ran over it," Bob responded, "but I won't let this one out and I'll change the cat box and I'll feed it . . . and everything . . ."

"Before we get attached to it, let's just let the poor little thing find a better home. We don't have the space or the time to train another cat right now. I know Daddy will agree with me." Mother's mind was made up.

"No more cats for a while," Mother had said. "We love them, and when they get out and get killed it is like losing a member of the family." She had said it, and she meant it. Now, with Dad's agreement, the cat could be put back outside.

Daddy stared hard at the black-and-white striped kitten snuggled under Bob's chin. When it came to cats, the boy was like a magnet. With very little coaxing, he could be the pied piper, leading all the cats in town.

"Son, if we let you keep this cat, you won't bring home anymore, will you?" Dad asked.

"Now Jeff, we don't need this one, much less anymore. We agreed. Remember?"

"Grace, the children don't have a place to play, and a cat is a clean pet once it's trained," Dad began.

Mother took the kitten from Bob and began a preliminary examination. "We don't know what kind of diseases this poor little thing may have, but one thing it has plenty of is fleas. It is crawling with a whole well-fed colony of them. Bob, you have a flea on your neck and—oh my, get upstairs, get your clothes off and take a soapy bath."

"But, but—can we keep him?"

"The kitten is skin and bones and besides carrying fleas, you could take no telling what from it. Be sensible, both of you. Put the poor little thing out—now—for goodness sake!" Mother loved cats as much as we did, but she was in no mood to housebreak another kitten.

"Well, then," Bob pleaded, "let's just feed him. He looks so hungry." As if in cahoots with Bob, the kitten meowed pitifully, pleading in a shaky little voice.

"If we feed him, he is our cat for good. I know cats. Feed a cat, keep a cat. He will never leave," lectured Mother, but she could see it was a losing battle. The pitiful, tiny kitten had made its appeal, and she loved animals. "All right! All right! But I will wish a thousand times I had never done this!"

Bob was scratching both his neck and ear, unaware of his activity as he smiled up at Mother.

"You get a bath while I start with the cat," Mother commanded.

Later, while the kitten clawed, Mother washed it in warm soapy water. Drying it in a soft towel, she put it in a large cardboard box and covered it for its period of confinement. "No sense letting the poor little thing bring in fleas. We have other things to do rather than de-flea the whole house." The kitten was purring contentedly after a bowl of milk. "Probably the first good meal it's had since its mother left it."

Mother had done a brief examination to confirm our new pet was a "he." A female cat meant more "blessed events" than the neighborhood needed. Our one and only veterinarian turned his attention toward cattle and horses and didn't often have time for or patience with small animal problems.

By nightfall we had the bad news. The soapy bath had removed only the obvious fleas. This cat had a case unrivaled in Mother's memory.

"But you can fix 'em, Mom, can't you?" Bob confidently asked.

"Yes, honey. But the kitty won't like it one bit. The fleas will be gone, but we won't get much sleep tonight."

"What is the magic cure for fleas?" I asked.

"A good dose of sulphur and lard," she answered.

"Are you kidding? That will kill the poor little thing," I cried.

I'm not feeding it to him. I'm rubbing it on the outside," Mother laughed. "No flea can survive that application."

"The cat can?" I wondered.

"Oh yes, but that doesn't mean he will like it. Come morning, no fleas will exist. Many's the time I've taken them off our dogs on the farm that way. It stinks and looks awful, but it works."

Mother was right on every count. That included the prophecy of no sleep. The kitten spent the night in a securely covered box and his black-and-white stripes were a gooey yellow stinky grease, but by morning the fleas were gone. After a more than thorough soapy warm bath, with several rinsings of warm water, he was a clean and much happier cat. In a couple of months, with regular feeding and careful care, he was a happy and beautiful one.

"Snoopy" moved into our house and into our hearts, and once the lights were out, into my bed. He became my regular bedfellow. Mother didn't like it. She still wasn't sure a cat wouldn't "draw a baby's breath away." But I wasn't a baby. Snoopy was. He was my baby. While Mother lectured "there would be no cats in bed at night," Snoopy lay innocently across the room curled into a comfortable ball. Once the lights were out, he jumped onto the foot of my bed. As I raised the covers with my foot, he crawled underneath and nosed his way up to the pillow beside mine. After gently biting my nose, he got his usual rubdown, then as he cradled his head on the pillow next to mine, I covered him up to his neck. And there he slept every night.

"Now, Norene, if you keep sleeping with that cat, you may develop an allergy to him. Get him out of that bed and keep him out," Mother worried. But I didn't. Her prophecy came true; I developed an almost deadly allergy to cat hair that exists to this day. However, it didn't happen for a long time, and Snoopy continued to be "found" every morning sleeping like the beautiful gentleman cat he would become on the pillow next to mine.

True to form, another kitten followed Bob home. As he gently stroked the yellow cat and cradled it in his arms, he innocently explained how it followed him until he finally took mercy on it. The ritual was almost an exact rerun of Snoopy's adoption process. However, Fluffy's fleas became discouraged after a couple of warm soapings and clear-water rinsings. Then we had a playful pair of kittens who kept us entertained, even into the wee hours of the night.

Although Snoopy still slept with me, he made exits several times at night for a midnight or early morning romp with Fluffy. They became quite a pair after the lights were out.

Bob and I enjoyed the midnight-chase-sneak-attacks they played on each other, usually after Daddy and Mother were asleep. Snoopy would stealthily crawl from his pillow and wait in anticipation for Fluffy to walk past the bed. Then he would pounce. Fluffy would meow in fright, and the race would begin. Across the floor into the living room, back across the sofa, and finally at top speed, directly across Mother and my peacefully snoring father.

Dad would have just gotten his best midnight snore up to full speed and shifted into overdrive when the cat brigade would pass across him at full tilt. Sucking in several man-sized snores without exhaling, Dad would strangle on his own vocal handiwork. Sitting straight up in bed as the kittens romped through a return engagement of their trailblazing effort, Dad would yell, "What in the Sam Hill was it?" while Bob and I screamed in laughter. By that time we would be standing at the foot of their bed, thoroughly engrossed in the midnight cat show.

After a good laugh, we would all settle down again to enjoy a much calmer night's sleep. Laughter proved to be a great relaxer.

The delightful little pair, however, were not destined to remain together. One afternoon, Fluffy saw the door open and made a hasty exit. Although we looked for our beautiful yellow half-grown kitten, he never returned. We ran an ad in the local newspaper, but nothing happened. Fluffy was gone.

Snoopy was pitifully lonely. He would walk through the house meowing as if calling his playmate. Each time he began his desolate hunt, our hearts joined his in missing Fluffy. We had lost a member of our family. We all missed the laughter and excitement of their playfulness.

Snoopy matured into a large, full-grown, well-petted cat. He continued to sleep with me just as he had before. After the lights were out, I waited for him to jump into the bed and nose his way under the covers to his pillow and purr his way to sleep. He never disappointed me. He was always there—until the night he got sick.

Snoopy slept fitfully that night, and I noticed his paws

felt hot and his nose was dry. Finally, I awakened Mother. "Snoopy is acting strangely."

Mother got up and looked him over. "Norene, Snoopy is sick. I don't know what is wrong with him, but you shouldn't be sleeping with him. He has a high fever. No telling what he has. I'll get a little basket, put a couple of soft towels in it, and put it by your bed. He can sleep there."

"Oh, he won't stay in a basket. He always sleeps with me," I told her, but I was wrong. Snoopy was so sick he didn't make any effort to move. I didn't sleep much more that night.

Snoopy was my special baby, and he didn't look very well. First we had lost Fluffy, and we just could not lose Snoopy, too. By morning he could not raise his head.

I wanted to call the veterinarian, but Mother was sure it wouldn't do any good. He only doctored large animals, anyway. She gave him some aspirin, crushed in water, in a spoon. She opened his mouth and poured it down his throat. Poor Snoopy was so sick, he hardly moved.

Two days passed. Snoopy lay in his basket, curled up in a lifeless heap. He drank only what Mother poured down his throat and not all of that. She kept giving him baby aspirin. Occasionally, he would stir, but mostly he lay lifeless in his basket. Bob and I couldn't look at him without crying. Four or five days—it seemed like an eternity—passed. Daddy became worried that Bob or I would find him dead. Mother said it was just a matter of time.

One day, in desperation Mother went into action. If Snoopy was going to die anyway, she had to be sure she had done everything possible to save him. Believing as she did in a clean system, she brought in the bottle of Milk of Magnesia. I protested some, but doing anything represented hope. He wasn't improving on his own. While I held Snoopy in my arms, Mother managed to feed him some of the medicine. For the most part, it just trickled down his throat. She washed his face with a warm wet washcloth, and tucked him back into his basket.

As soon as I got home from school, I rushed in to inspect the kitty basket. Snoopy was sitting up. He looked a bit dazed and very weak, but his eyes were open and he was interested in finding his cat box.

From that moment on, he continued to improve. In a few days he was his old self. It was then we noticed that his front legs were slightly bowed.

"The poor thing. Looks a little like a bull dog," I commented.

"It must have been caused by the high fever," Mother explained.

What had bowed his front legs didn't matter. Snoopy was well and soon again was sleeping with his head on his pillow next to mine.

We told the story often. Mother maintained that cats are just like people: they need their systems cleaned out every so often. I wasn't so sure. But Snoopy lived to be a beautiful old bowlegged, often-petted, well-loved cat.

THE FLOOD

IT HAD BEEN A WET SPRING, EXCEPTION-
ally wet. More rain had fallen than many people could
ever remember. One storm had followed another until
blue sky and sunshine were dim memories.

The creeks, rivers, and roads were brimful. There was
no room for another cupful anywhere, and it was still
raining. Then the news came. The river was going to crest
that night at twelve feet above flood level. We waited in
disbelief.

Downtown was a mile or more from the river, and the
talk was that it would "take a lot of water before it
reached us." The town's park had disappeared. Travel
north of town was cut off.

By seven it was time for me to go to work at the movie
theater. I had been the ticket taker and popcorn salesper-
son nightly and on weekends since starting high school.

A phone call had verified the movie would be open
regardless of the weather forecast. Water wouldn't get
into town, the theater manager assured us, so we went on
about our soggy lives, inconvenienced but not threatened. Besides, the movie theater was less than a block
from my dad's café.

The evening began calmly enough. We opened the theater for business, made popcorn, and prepared for a regular evening. But it was not to be. After a few customers
came, we started the show. Then the girl in the ticket

booth came out to tell us water was curb high. The manager had called to say we should turn on the lights and announce that Main Street was flooded and the water was still rising.

By the time our few moviegoers had reclaimed their money, the water was covering half of the sidewalk. The theater owner had found some boards somewhere and had attempted to barricade the swinging doors on either side of the ticket booth. But holding back the tide was impossible.

The barricade of old towels and small rugs stuffed around the boards only lasted a few minutes. Slowly at first, small rivulets of water crept across the floor and into the carpeting. The rivulets quickly turned to mounds of mush as water gushed on into the theater. The sloping floor inside was a welcome avenue for swirling mud and water. In no time we were standing ankle deep in water inside the lobby.

"Look! There are boats on Main Street!" Jackie, our cashier, shouted. Sure enough, two metal fishing boats sputtered past the windows.

"Catching anything, fellows?" someone shouted.

"Yeah, a bunch of wisecracks! Are you people okay, or do you need a ride outta here?"

In the meantime, Daddy had called to say he would be around to walk me home. The water was deep, but he was sure we could make it.

Jackie and our manager accepted rides since water in the street was nearly waist high on an adult. As Daddy and I linked arms and stepped over the barriers, water tugged at our legs. The mud under our feet seemed to form a sticky glue.

"That is rich topsoil you feel under your feet," Daddy said. "There is more than one way to lose a farm."

As we turned the corner to the café, the current became

more swift and the swirling water caught at my skirt. By the time we reached the bottom of the rickety stairway leading upstairs, I was aware of my skirt continually slipping down. Each time I readjusted it with greater effort.

A careful inventory upstairs, a few minutes later, revealed that in the short walk home I had completely lost a frilly half slip and had mangled and torn my skirt.

That was one of the few times I was glad we lived on the second floor. Ugly or not, it was dry and safe. Few places in downtown, and the majority of residential neighborhoods, could claim that distinction.

By early morning the water had begun to recede, leaving a heavy coat of the sticky topsoil Dad had observed the night before.

For at least two days, Mother and Dad scooped mud and washed floors in the café. It was a mess, but a mess not nearly on the scale of the theater where watersoaked carpeting molded and soured. All the water down front had to be pumped out, which took extra time. The entire inside of the building had to be redecorated before people could come and not be driven out by the smell. The following two weeks were hectic. Painting waterlogged surfaces was futile, so things had to completely dry out before the repair work could begin.

Finally, the last of the mud was scooped, swept, and washed away. Floors were recarpeted or refinished, walls painted, and several windows and doors replaced.

Main Street returned to normal, but our frightening memories lingered. The conversation always started about the same way: "Do you remember the night motor boats took over Main Street?"

And if the answer was "yes," the reminiscing lasted for hours.

THE TUBA

THE WALK TO AND FROM SCHOOL WAS A
ritual, a social happening of sorts. Who walked home
with whom and what was said and to whom were discussed and analyzed over the phone between friends
every night. Indeed, this mundane, daily happening was
more than a journey. In its own way it could have been a
small town version of *The Canterbury Tales*.

Those two-block walks from the school to Main Street
shaped our outlooks, helped mold friendships, and
formed our social history. Since I was several years older,
I was in high school when my little brother was in grade
school. However, he was large for his age and was perfectly capable of carrying the high school tuba while still
in the lower grades.

When he was asked to play the tuba at such a tender
age, his enthusiasm and dedication overwhelmed my
parents but thoroughly embarrassed me. He lovingly carried that oversized foghorn home every day, and in doing
so he put a cramp in my homegoing flirtations and social
life.

The first time I heard that tuneless toot-toot-toot, done
to the cadence of a bass drum somewhere behind me, I
froze. Surely God was not going to allow that inspired
child to make me the laughingstock of the entire high
school crowd. I believed in poetic justice, and I was a
good person deserving of my dignity. Likewise, Dad was

an upright individual who could put a stop to such indignities raining down upon my head.

"Norene, is that your little brother practicing the tuba again?" The remarks grew worse as the year advanced.

Dad was always quick to point out how proud he was of his young son. "There are a lot worse things a child could do on the way home," he would say. One comment infuriated me more than all the others: "As long as he is playing that horn, we know where he is!"

Yeah, I knew where he was all right. And so did the whole town.

"But Daddy, can't he just carry the darned thing and practice when he gets home?" I pleaded.

"He isn't hurting anybody," Dad explained patiently. "Leave the little fellow alone. You are the only one who even notices it."

I noticed it all right—every morning and afternoon! And I dreaded it.

"Hey, Norene, that relative of yours always furnishes us traveling music!"

"Tell us what he's playing. Is that a tune or the world's greatest source of natural gas?"

The remarks never ceased. Neither did the eternal tooting. My each and every word seemed punctuated by a toot.

"What—toot—are—toot—you—toot—doing—toot— tonight?" When he was immediately behind us, the words had to come between these short explosions to be understood. I prayed Bob would fall on his horn and smash it or get too close to the railroad tracks, drop it, and a train would run over it—or anything that would stop his "practicing his way" to school and back.

Providence didn't provide such a lasting answer to prayer, but there was one nearly successful interlude. That afternoon during the tooting trip home, an unfor-

gettable incident finally occurred that was worthy of
Dad's attention. As Bob was tooting along in his own
world of "big bands on the march," he had tooted his way
past me and my friends and overtaken a frail senior
citizen on her way home from the grocery store. Since her
hearing was almost gone, she was also in a world of her
own. Slowly puttering down the sidewalk, feebly clutching her small sacks of groceries, she was blissfully unaware of the mighty blowhard marching behind her and
gaining ground.

Slowly, deliberately, the defenseless little old lady
crossed the sidewalk and was making preparations to
step from the curb to the street. Meanwhile, the fearless
bandsman marched victoriously down the middle of the
walk tooting as he came.

Suddenly he was even with the unsuspecting octoge-
narian. As she insecurely searched for that first step off
the curb, Bob reached deep within his diaphragm to
produce the mightiest toot of his budding career. Jerking
with the shock of probably the first real sound she had
heard in years, she jolted upright. Grocery sacks shot
from her arms into the street, and she settled limply into
the gutter among her groceries and now-empty sacks, her
hat askew on her snow-white hair. Unaware of the drama
unfolding at his feet, Bob marched bravely on.

Other people along the sidewalk and several from inside neighboring stores came to the rescue of the dishev-
eled but unhurt old lady. She was helped to her feet,
her groceries gathered into the sacks again, and her dignity slowly restored. The vocal reassurances and relieved
laughter that followed were blissfully accompanied by
the receding cadence of the tuba fading into the distance
around the corner.

My imagination was fully fired. My instincts were
screaming "Kill" as I rushed home. I was ready to paint a

violent word-picture of a horn-blowing monster marching blindly across the body of a weak, defenseless crea-
ture unable to protect herself. Justice had been served,
and I was ready to report it!

Nor was I lacking in inspiration. I was like a plaintiff's
criminal lawyer at a murder trial, ready to mesmerize the
jury with my final summation and demand the death
penalty.

I burst through the café door shouting, "Daddy, do you
know what Bob just did?"

Dad listened quietly. However, as I poured description
on top of description, his jaw set firmly and his blue eyes
hardened. I did well. My imagery-laden rhetoric would
have stirred any crowd to riot.

"Bob's horn is history," I thought proudly. His career as
a foghorn tooter is dust. Peace and quiet will reign once
more on my walk to and from school, and he will fade
into obscurity where he belongs, just another face in the
crowd. I stood there relishing the richness of the moment.

"Is this all true, son?" Dad began.

"I—I—don't think so, sir. I didn't see any old lady. I
didn't step on anybody."

I gloated as his confusion increased. Dad made some
calls to the store owners on Main Street. Each apparently
verified my story but assured Dad the lady hadn't been
hurt, just a little surprised, shocked, and shaken. She was
safely home now with no damage done.

Finally satisfied, Dad turned to us. Bob was not to play
his horn on the street until he could learn to watch where
he was going. Horn playing was suspended for the time
being. However, I was not to stretch my stories, insinuate
unsubstantiated circumstances, or be the family tattle-
tale.

My pride was momentarily wounded. I was the de-
fender of justice, and it had not been duly served. Bob

was getting off too easy. Fortunately I had the good sense not to talk back. The look on Daddy's normally smiling face was stern, and I knew from past experience the value of silence at such times.

It wasn't long before Bob was happily tooting to and from school again and my life was being noisily accompanied by the town's most inspired tuba player.

It was probably all for the best. Bob tooted his way through college and has been a successful high school band director for years.

THE WEDDING

HIGH SCHOOL GIRLS WIELDING COMBS and compacts gathered together in a growing, giggling cluster around mirrors in the girls' bathroom before school. Lipstick inscriptions in vivid colors screamed "Bobby Ray loves Rita Fay" and "Kilroy was here" from corners of the recently polished glass.

"Oh, he is so cute."

"What did you do last night?"

"Well, I heard . . ."

"We are going."

"Robert Carol said he did!"

Conversation gushed in an ever-mounting crescendo as more girls pushed through the doors to check their hair for the first class.

"Mary Louise, is that a diamond on your left hand?" someone squealed. The conversational uproar turned to screams as a normally quiet girl with long reddish-brown hair held out a pretty manicured hand displaying a new engagement ring.

"When did you get it?"

"Did you know he was giving it to you?"

"How romantic!"

"When are you getting married?"

"Are you having a church wedding?"

Questions came steadily, along with squeals of delight,

as the knot of girls tightened with excited demands of "Let me see."

Mary Louise, a high school junior, was sixteen years old. Few people in our crowd thought about her age. Marriage came early in this farming community where romantic ideals, early responsibility, and hard work replaced college, especially for girls. The reigning philosophy was that girls didn't need to go to college. They were to be wives, homemakers, and eventually mothers, anyway. If a girl went to college, she went as a home economics major. Anything else was a waste of time. Of course, a girl could become a teacher, but she might not get married if she did. And who wanted to be an old maid? In Mary Louise's case, the problem was solved early.

Three weeks later, wedding invitations were in the mail. As was customary with big church weddings, additional invitations were pinned on bulletin boards of all churches in town, and church bulletins had printed copies of them prominently displayed inside in case anyone had been overlooked.

Luncheons and parties were punctuated by bridal showers until the bride was too tired to get married and we were too tired to attend. Weddings, and the excitement they generated, rivaled only Christmas.

The entire community came to the wedding, and the church was full. Those arriving late stood in the back, but no one went home.

There wasn't room for everything: people, flowers, and wedding party. Flowers were everywhere. The altar was covered. Bouquets gushed from windows, and beribboned nosegays cascaded over ends of pews down the center aisle. The bride's parents had bought out the florists' shops. Rumor was that two extra truckloads of flowers and greenery had been delivered special from Oklahoma

City that day. The sanctuary looked and smelled like an overstuffed, well-fertilized forest.

In spite of two large bridal showers, more gifts filled the foyer where they were stacked in higgledy-piggledy fashion on tables and overflowed onto surrounding floor space. Custom bows and professional wrappings suffered crush fatigue, as did guests and the wedding party.

The church was medium-sized, but the wedding was meant for a cathedral. The community royalty came but couldn't sit down. They brought gifts, but there was inadequate space for them. Large flower bouquets, baskets of flowers, and palm trees were added to flower trees and candle trees. Only a machete skillfully used with large sweeping strokes would have cleared enough space for all the wedding party.

As the bridesmaids began their descent down the aisle in twos, eight of them preceded the ringbearer and flower girl. Organ music swelled as eight groomsmen, eight bridesmaids, and two baby members of the party wedged themselves into the flower undergrowth.

Palm trees twitched, flower trees wiggled, and the candle trees tilted as members of the wedding came to roost. Finally the music crescendoed, and sixteen-year-old Mary Louise swept down the aisle in her *Gone With the Wind* wedding dress. It was the biggest day of her life, and her parents had ordered the whole catalog.

The bride's father was an afterthought since there wasn't room for both him and the dress side by side. The groom had taken his place in front of the floral jungle. He extended his hand to the bride, and that was as close as he was going to get.

The bride's father shouted, "Her mother and I do," from up the aisle somewhere when the question of "Who gives this bride?" was posed.

The best man held fast to the back of the ringbearer's

coat collar because the little fellow's response wasn't always dependable. Once the rings were dispersed, the tiny boy's real personality surfaced.

Free of rings, the pillow took flight as the little bearer sailed it into the audience and ran squealing to his mother.

"I was good, I was good," he sang. "Now do I get my new scooter? Do I?"

The audience laughed, and the ceremony continued. With another song and another prayer, the bride and groom knelt on the white satin bench, but it was not gracefully done. The bride lacked experience maneuvering long skirts of hundreds of yards of material. The large wire hoops that held them out were an added burden. As she struggled to a kneeling position, her knees came to rest on the largest hoop. It responded to the pressure placed there and the back side of the large, sturdy hoop became airborne, taking yards of material up with it.

When the young couple finally reached their knees the audience and the inspired photographer were treated to a rare sight seldom seen at any wedding—the beautiful see-through lace underwear of the bride. As the hardy hoop sprang into action, propelled in front by the bride's knees, the rear end crept upward, suddenly revealing a most intimate view of her very private and skimpily clad behind!

The audience gasped, then giggled, and the photographer raced up the aisle snapping as he went. Seeing the bride's head encircled in the largest wedding dress in history, the minister quickly pled God's blessing and brought the sideshow presentation to an end. However, it was not soon enough to spare the bride the most embarrassing moment of her life. She had felt the rush of air on her almost bare posterior and had guessed the rest, but she was powerless to gain control. Fate had seen fit to leave her provocatively clad rear end bare to ridicule.

The much-needed prayer ended. With help from the groom and maid of honor, the abused hoop dress finally settled back into place. The couple were pronounced man and wife, but not nearly soon enough.

A massive eight-layer cake with stanchions in between was soon cut, and the couple left on their honeymoon trip. The altar revelation stayed well behind.

For years after that, when anyone mentioned a wedding, the story was trotted out and retold. Each time the dress got fuller, the hoop got bigger, and the bride's underwear continued to shrink.

Shock was followed by waves of grief two weeks later when the young bride and groom returned from their honeymoon. All was well when they got home, but Mary Louise complained of being tired and went into her room to rest while supper was being prepared. When her mother went to awaken her, she was dead.

At sixteen she had died of heart failure, an enlarged heart that had gone undetected. The shock of her death sent the community reeling in disbelief.

Married only two weeks earlier in a fairy tale wedding in the dress of almost any girl's dreams, her life had just suddenly stopped.

The young groom and the families were grief-stricken. Just as the community had celebrated their happiness, it now grieved their loss.

The same church that had been too small to hold the wedding could not contain the mourners for the funeral. Again the flowers filled the altar, the aisles, and the windows, but the bouquets were much more solemn. The casket was decked in pink roses, the spray reminiscent of the bridal bouquet.

The entire high school student body attended. The same girls who had squealed in innocent wonder over the engagement ring and gasped in teenage delight at the bride as she glided down the aisle wept openly now at her death.

Mary Louise was buried in her wedding dress and veil. The lower half of the casket was covered in a much larger bouquet than she had carried only two weeks earlier.

The minister who had performed the wedding spoke the words of comfort to the same audience. Sobs punctuated the organ background as the heavy scent of the funeral flowers set the mood for a final goodbye.

The distraught groom, along with members of his family and the bride's family, sat together on the first two rows. Tears were not enough; words were inadequate.

Our grief flowed together as we reached out to each other in that moment of bereavement. A young love so recently begun in moments of beauty, merriment, and embarrassment, now so suddenly ended with dreams unfulfilled. It left our hearts hollow. We cried together for each other, for ourselves, and for this couple who could not continue.

Later, we huddled together at the gravesite. There were more tears, more words, more music. And the sea of flowers from the church transferred our material expressions of anguish to the cemetery.

Music Lesson

SHE TAUGHT PIANO, AND HER PERFECTED southern drawl made it clear she was from New Orleans. She was overpoweringly large to her small pupils. Her off-key sing-song of "One anda two anda three" was punctuated with the occasional crack of a ruler across the knuckles of a young protégé. "Curve ya fingers" was added in a shout but kept in time with the continuing "One anda two anda." The slap of the ruler never really hurt, but it did its share to unnerve the future concert pianist at her side. When not in use as a weapon, the ruler was employed as a pointer to the note to follow.

When the note duly pointed out failed to follow, because of confusion or ignorance, the instruction continued always in time. "Next note anda three anda foura."

The instruction "next note anda two anda" didn't always produce results. When that occurrence presented itself, the note was inserted in the counting cadence "two anda C-flat anda foura anda. . . ."

Quite often the greatest number of notes played came from her mouth and not the small musician's fingers. However, her counting seldom stopped until the half-hour period was observed and ended punctually with the ringing of the old alarm clock on top of the piano. The clock was set at the beginning of each lesson.

"We don't want to go ova'time, hea'," she would explain at the end of the half-hour.

If one of us played unusually well, we were sent to wash our hands with soap and given the seat of honor at her shiny black baby grand piano in her unused, over-crowded living room. The next pupil to arrive observed the splendid performance, and the time was deducted from his half-hour!

"We must be inspired by this lovely performance now, mustn't we?" Then, in several years that student would be allowed to touch the grand piano if he ever played so well or lived so long. Few ever did. The provokingly poor student who lacked knowledge and inspiration seldom finished the lesson. Instead, he paid his money and tackled the constant mound of dirty dishes in the teacher's overcrowded sink.

Lenelle, a girlfriend of mine, washed dishes often while I took part of the piano time her money covered. She hated doing dishes at home, but paying for the privilege was even less sporting. Lenelle's music career was short-lived.

I enjoyed those days. Occasionally, in her disgust, Lenelle dropped some fragile china on the floor, bringing a reprimand from the piano.

"Ca'ful in thaya anda two anda . . ." the teacher would shout in a steady, Bach-like cadence.

Lenelle soon stopped taking music since it resulted only in dishpan hands, but for a while she kept accompanying me to lessons. That, too, was short-lived because this teacher had Lenelle permanently cast in her mind as a maid. She was sent to wash dishes whether she paid for the privilege or not. Thereafter, our friendship was placed on hold during piano lesson time.

Mrs. DuBeaux obviously liked me, perhaps not because of my musical talent so much as the amount of sheet music I bought. On rare days after a lesson I was even given a ride back to town in her shiny blue antique Ford. Although it was nearly twenty years old, the upholstery still smelled new. The car was in mint condition. It was like the grand piano—unused. To ride in it, the feet and shoes were washed in addition to the hands being washed with soap and water, then dried. Then the heavy lock came off the garage, and the new twenty-year-old Ford with the new smell inside was meticulously backed out from the garage and the student allowed to board. However, even with clean hands we weren't allowed to touch the door or upholstery.

"The awl in the body, you unda'stand," she'd state firmly.

The rides were as rare as touching the grand piano. Such privileges occurred only on sunny days. The car was never removed from the garage on rainy ones.

Few students continued to study the piano with her much past the third or fourth grade. Several excuses were given.

"So few truly talented children exist today, except, of course, in Baton Rouge" was often the reason given by her. However, those hardy few of us who did continue knew the real reason. A growing student soon could no longer share the bench with the teacher's well-fed bulk. We, the few determined, hardy souls, often laughed about "hanging on." We not only learned to play the piano, but we did it the hard way—balancing carefully in thin air! That balancing act rarely produced outstanding music. When we finally claimed the entire piano bench, in public, for ourselves at the once-a-year recitals, the full view of the keyboard and a completely steady seat beneath us often produced some surprising results!

Owning the entire piano bench didn't free us from the counting procedure. From backstage or the baptistry, if the recital was held in the Baptist Church, would come the hissing sounds of "one anda two anda, continue to the next page, one anda two anda . . ."

We often laughed at the lady's enormous size but not out loud. Not until a particular small-town society Christmas party where several piano students were to perform.

All of the invited guests were seated at wobbly card tables draped in red-and-green tablecloths and candlelit. We were served wartime rations of one slender finger sandwich, a thin cookie, and a tiny cup of red Christmas punch with a mint leaf floating on the top. Such a scarcity of food had obviously not been a part of Mrs. DuBeaux's upbringing, putting aside the myth that she had viewed parts of the Civil War from her Baton Rouge bedroom window.

Several times this southern paragon of enlarged loveliness had highly praised the tasty offerings on her plate and was given refills for her trouble. However, the fourth and fifth round of compliments were rewarded with icy stares by the hostess. But a battle was taking place in Mrs. DuBeaux's mind between her impeccable southern manners and her gnawing hunger. The war within was quick and terrible. The physical demands of hunger won.

Not to be starved in the midst of one of her own programs, Mrs. DuBeaux rose from her relieved, creaking party chair to serve herself. On her way to a standing position, the wobbly card table became attached to her oversized stomach. Red punch, punch cups, half-eaten cookies, and leftover sandwiches washed to the downside of the now upended card table and deposited portions of themselves on three surprised table companions, staining dresses and dousing holiday hairdos. As Mrs. DuBeaux had stood, the table appeared to go up with her, then release itself squarely on her three unprotected table mates.

"Oh dea'," she shouted defensively, while furiously dabbing at her own unscathed party dress with a tiny napkin.

Pandemonium reigned as we grasped the situation in

progress. In the effort to dodge a few flying cups and saucers, other tables were upended. The once-peaceful scene could have been any out-West saloon brawl after a raid and a shootout by the local sheriff. Tables, cups, saucers, leftover red punch, tablecloths, and a rain of crumbs seemed to hang for a minute in midair amid screams and mad dashes toward the door.

We were free to leave. The party was canceled without further notice as the hostess flew around sopping up bright red puddles of punch from her white carpet.

"The old pig," I heard the irate hostess mutter in spite of herself. "Next time she can bring a sack lunch," mumbled the distraught lady while mopping furiously at the permanently stained carpet.

This story was added to many others that periodically made the rounds when some former pupil would bring up Mrs. DuBeaux's name. Perhaps it was remembrances of that musical background that spared me the pain of teaching music. Remembering the "one anda two andas" made me sure I never wanted to take her place on the other end of that piano bench.

July Fourth

THE FOURTH OF JULY WAS A BIG HOLI-
day in our small community. It served as a time for family
reunions and picnics in the park. Small-town businesses
closed, and everyone took the day off. The young people
usually celebrated by leaving town because there was
"nothing to do," not for ages fourteen to twenty-two.

Because food meant food talk—"Grace, your rolls are
the best. Does it really take all night to make them?"—
such penetrating conversations just weren't young folks'
choice of entertainment. It held no thrill somehow.

Just the anticipation of the smells of that season gave
some dyed-in-the-wool Southerners indigestion early.
The Fourth was a reunion of southern food, more food
than a small nation would need to reverse a famine.
Those jealously guarded creations came in boxes, crates,
picnic baskets, and cake and pie carriers.

"Be careful, Lem. That's Emma Fay's special impossible
cake. Just you crack the icing, and you'll be buried in an
unmarked grave."

Ceremony marked the unveiling of each well-known
dish. Once "laid out," that sea of food was the main
attraction. The women arranged the display while the
men watched, anticipation etched on their faces.

"You can gain weight just lookin'." There were salads:
green leafy salads, main-dish salads, and jellied salads;
casseroles: varied vegetable casseroles, scalloped corn

casseroles, even scalloped oyster casseroles; there were puddings of every variety; and potatoes: smooth mashed, German mashed, potato salad, and scalloped potatoes. If it happened to a potato, it was there. But centering it all were the mountains of fried chicken, each bowlful a sacred recipe passed down from generation to generation like a birthright. And gravy, oceans of gravies, to complement the fried chicken of choice.

"When I die, Grace, I hope I do it in a pan of your gravy!" someone told Mother. Then there was pecan pie, miles of it, sporting enough calories to put the entire American army on the march. "The Fourth" was food, unforgettable food.

"Everybody is going to Oklahoma City on the Fourth, Mom."

"Not everybody. You aren't." As far as Mother was concerned, the subject was closed. Saying anymore would have equated talking back or being sassy, so the only other avenue was a sincere appeal to Dad. That had to be carefully approached since he prided himself on upholding Mother's discipline. In fact, the mental and emotional hopscotch of each one of them leaving the decision to the other often canceled out an otherwise perfectly good idea, and at age sixteen I was longing for more freedom.

"I don't know, honey. What did your mother say?"

"Have you asked Daddy?"

"Your mother usually has some thoughts on things like that. Have you asked her?"

The pathway between those two opinions could become threadbare before a decision was reached, but to go anywhere out of town without the okay of both parents was unthinkable and unacceptable. I often lamented that by the time they had arrived at a positive conclusion, I was too tired to go anyway. But after all that mental agony, I'd rise to the occasion or die trying!

When I casually mentioned the idea to Dad, he quickly quoted highway death predictions for the upcoming holiday. I was dead, and the holiday had not even dawned yet! Well, my idea was dead, and I might as well be.

If I had to stay home that day, I was sentenced to both boredom and embarrassment. Mother and Dad would take my little brother to the park, and the day would be spent with old people and little kids. Some little old lady wearing hearing aids in both ears would ask too loudly, "Why didn't you go out of town with all the other young people this weekend?"

The whole park full of people would stop talking. Even babies would stop crying, waiting for my answer.

"My parents wouldn't let me. There are going to be five million deaths on the highways this weekend and my parents didn't want to send me to an early grave."

Then the whole park full of people would gasp in shock since Daddy was the only man in town aware of the national statistics on traffic deaths.

"I remember one Fourth of July back when I was a girl. . . ." the stone-deaf old hag would screech at three times the volume of necessary sound. I would be stuck there in the middle of the city park between the yelling babies and the residents of the old folks' home for the rest of my life. And I would be buried there, my face beet-red with frustration. I would be buried at the entrance to the park, and my tombstone would read "Died of Embarrassment on July Fourth, a Holiday Statistic."

All that kept me from dying so early in my youth was an idea I didn't even think of. The guy who had asked me was a few years older than I was, and he had the good sense to stop by and ask Mom and Dad if I could go.

"Such a nice young man, so responsible," Mother purred and gave her consent.

"I know she wants to go," Daddy had added, "and I'll feel better knowing you are driving. Be careful and have a good time."

In Oklahoma City four of us attacked the park on that holiday and rode everything. The third consecutive trip on the big roller coaster nearly made me a statistic, not the traffic or the accidents. We didn't see any accidents. But it was the scene that greeted us when we got home that left a lasting impression.

The hearse, our small-town answer to an ambulance, was just unloading Mother. She had a cast on her right leg all the way up her thigh, and she was still in pain.

While I had braved the holiday crowds and defied the nation's statistics, Mother had spent a safe Fourth of July in the park where she had fallen off the merry-go-round and broken her leg.

I immediately saw the humor in it all. She never did.

THE KISS

"**D**ADDY, DADDY. I'M IN A HURRY!" I WHIS-
pered desperately.

He was either ignoring me or immensely engrossed in
his conversation with the man sitting on the stool next to
him at the counter.

"Psssst, Daddy" I shouted in a stage whisper.

That got his attention, and he turned around. The man
next to him sipped his coffee, looking in the other direction.

"Honey, I'm talking business here. What do you need?"
Dad inquired with a hint of impatience.

"My good-bye kiss. You always kiss me 'bye when I
leave. I've kissed Mother and—"

"You will have to excuse me this time, honey. I'm busy.
You go on this morning, and I'll kiss you when you get
home," he instructed, turning to resume his interrupted
conversation.

Confused, I stood there. Daddy had always kissed me
good-bye when I left for school ever since I was little. It was
tradition, a ritual we observed, like prayer before meals
and brushing our teeth. It was something we "always" did,
a special salute that took place. If it was forgotten, we had
to return to square one and take care of it immediately. Not
kissing Dad good-bye was a "breach of etiquette." Unthinkable.

He was totally oblivious to me as I stood there looking

at his back. As he sat there on the stool, his head with its slick little bald spot was beckoning me—a little wickedly—with an idea. He wouldn't refuse to kiss me good-bye again!

I quickly opened my purse, sifted through the contents to find my lipstick, and applied a fresh and adequate supply. Approving of the bright, ruby-red mouth, I closed the case and stood on tiptoes, positioning myself so my well-outlined lips would land directly in the center of Dad's bald spot. Then I kissed him solidly and soundly on top of the head. His small rim of hair made a majestic frame for the telltale picture so grandly inscribed atop the shiny surface. I quietly surveyed my handiwork. No one could miss that vivid tattoo. They'd never dream it was the innocent work of a daughter—it was perfectly awful!

Had Dad not been such a solid citizen, the town gossips would have enjoyed an open season on speculation. As it was, everybody had a good laugh at his expense.

Ten o'clock was doughnut time townwide. Everybody up and down Main Street came to enjoy Mother's home-made doughnuts. All morning Daddy cared for the customers' needs at the counter. The town came, the town saw, the town laughed!

Daddy was only aware of roars of laughter each time he turned his back. Every time some new observer was treated to that provocative sight atop his head, the laughter increased. However, no one told him the problem. When he asked, the observers would shrug or shake their heads while continuing to giggle.

Desperate, Dad asked Mother to inspect him and find out what was so funny. As he turned around, she attempted to discover the mystery behind the giggling, but she didn't see anything wrong. Mother was barely five feet fall, while Daddy was over six feet.

The laughter continued to puzzle Daddy until just before noon when Elvina came to work. She took one look at Daddy and burst out laughing.

"What is it?" Dad's frustrated voice inquired. "All morning people have been laughing. For goodness' sake, help me out," he pleaded.

"You been like that all morning?" Elvina laughed.

"Yes," wailed Dad. "For goodness' sake, tell me."

"This is too much," giggled Elvina, wiping her eyes. "That rotten Norene must have kissed you on your bald head with her bright red lipstick. She sure planted one on you, too! If I didn't know you better, Jeff, I'd say you were a dirty ole man!"

Dad grabbed a small hand mirror and backed up to the large mirror back of the coffee urn. He stared in disbelief.

"That little rascal! I didn't kiss her good-bye this morning, and she really got even!" As he stared in the mirror, it got funnier, and his smile turned into laughter.

With Mother's help, Dad was able to wash the lipstick off before the high school kids got to the café for lunch. However, in spite of a standing-room-only crowd, he found me at the cash register.

"You surely got even with me for not kissing you good-bye this morning," he laughed, his face almost as red as the lipstick.

"Daddy, I couldn't leave without a kiss," I teased. "Did the coffee crowd get to admire it?"

"Oh, they admired it all right! And you know what, not one person would tell me why they were laughing. Not one! And poor Mother obviously couldn't see up that high!"

"No one told you?"

"Not until Elvina came to work."

"I love it! I really love it. My faith in the human race is restored," I giggled. "It really is! Oh, and Daddy, you owe me a kiss, remember?"

Daddy put his arms around me right there in front of the high school crowd and kissed me. Then we stood there with our arms around each other—laughing at our own foolishness.

THE SCHOOL CHOIR

EVERYDAY OCCURRENCES ARE MAGNIfied in a small community because that is all there is. The three most pivotal areas of our lives were our homes, churches, and schools. All other events were in some way interconnected, like spokes to the hub of a wheel.

The hiring of a new school superintendent was an important event, but he seemed rather removed from the lives of the students. Oh, we saw him attending meetings and civic clubs and making decisions of general policy, but the member of his family who touched our lives was his wife.

The Taylor family moved to our town from another one very much like it, just smaller. Mrs. Taylor taught vocal music, and she did it well. She was a beautiful woman with deep-set, expressive black eyes, creamy white skin, and jet-black hair. Her hands and eyes spoke eloquently of the art she loved. I often wondered if she was at the height of her happiness when she was teaching.

Although Mrs. Taylor's husband had improved his career with their move, she had left years of hard work behind her. Her choirs had won state competitions numerous times in the past. It was clear she wasn't inheriting a bargain when she got us; there was no comparison.

Not only was Mrs. Taylor a master of her art, but so was her sister. For a number of years they had brought their choirs to state championships and had faced each other in the final competitions. First and second places had usually belonged to the choral groups directed by these two women. Both of them were skilled artists of their crafts, and differences came only in the age and experience of the particular groups they directed in any given year.

"Are you joining choir this year?"

"I am. We will win state with Mrs. Taylor."

"Not this year we won't. We sound like a bunch of rusty hinges."

"Yeah, but she can fix us!"

"The poor woman isn't God, ya' know."

The general gossip before class set the tone for what was expected of her. For most of the students, it was Mrs. Taylor's job. Our giving anything toward expected success wasn't a consideration until choir period began.

It was clear from the beginning that the sloppy behavior of the past was just that—past!

"Stand tall, think tall, and vocalize."

We did, but not with enthusiasm. We wanted to sing real songs, but when she finally brought out the music, it wasn't the popular, well-known jukebox variety at all. It was difficult, and so were the attitudes of some of the choir members.

This wasn't fun anymore; it was hard work. This dynamic woman was relentless. It wasn't fair!

The day our first grades came out, mutiny was heavily considered on our walk back to Main Street after school.

"I made a lousy C in choir!"

"Is that the nerve? The woman expects us to read music. I can stand right here and name ten good country singers that make more'en her, and they can't read a note of music."

"Hope you've noticed she plays favorites."

"Ha! Who can miss it?"

The talk raged as disappointed, disgruntled choir members planned their strategy.

"Yeah, she likes Carolyn the best."

"That makes me mad. So Carolyn can sing. Big deal! Don't we all deserve an equal chance?"

But while students raved outside of class, we were afraid not to work when she faced us in the choir room and raised her baton. "Students, listen to each other as you sing. You are a part of the whole, not the whole itself. All of you are singing solos. Choir is dependent on a group effort. You are only as strong as your weakest member. Listen to each other. Help each other!"

But it was hard to change old ways. We improved that year, but feelings were bruised and jealousy festered for a future upheaval.

At state we sang better than we ever had, but it wasn't nearly good enough. The choir Mrs. Taylor's sister directed easily placed first. We were down the line somewhere. Their superior rating with commendation made our excellent rating look like a face with mud on its nose.

Mrs. Taylor kept smiling as she expressed her appreciation for our hard work on the bus home. And we had worked hard, very hard. We had sounded great in comparison with the previous year. One thing few of us missed was the obvious sadness deep within those black eyes. They spoke volumes.

The next year our attitudes were better. Those members who didn't like the hard work could quit—now. We passed the word. That didn't cure our lack of musical ability, but it helped. Also, several of us took private voice from her. That did work some magic.

Finally, a month before state she announced everyone had to have all music perfectly memorized, or they would be left at home. No music, no faking it, and no singing sour notes. Everyone had to listen as well as sing and hear the harmony as well as feel the time. She was having individual tryouts in two weeks.

"What? Tryouts? After a year's work, tryouts?"

"She's flipped her wig!"

Many of the regular members threatened to quit. A few did rather than face individual tryouts. The new tactics were the talk of the school. But they took place on time.

The choir that emerged was a little smaller, but every note and every word were perfected. However, we still were not equal to the top choral group of the past year. She didn't say that; we did among ourselves. Even in our final warm-up, as we prepared to sing in the state competition, that final delicacy of tone was not yet there.

Our opening note demanded a soft diminished chord that graduated into the full, rich roundness of tone sufficient to chase chills up our audience's spines. We wanted it to happen for Mrs. Taylor to show our love and appreciation for all she had done. We wanted to do it for us to prove that we could. But we really wanted to beat her sister!

We stood quietly in our places, our eyes on the glittering, expressive, jet-black eyes of our director. As the curtain opened, each of us grasped the fingers of the person on either side. One quick squeeze said, "This is it." As the curtain opened, Mrs. Taylor formed the words, "You will do it. Good luck!"

We leaned a little forward as a group, and for the first time our opening note was like a little crystal bell ringing somewhere in the distance. Holding the beauty of that faraway, bell-like quality, we gradually augmented into the mighty chorus we had become. Mrs. Taylor's eyes glistened with tears. We sang as we had never sung before, every eye on the beautiful lady in front of us. We were one voice.

The magic of the moment continued. The sound

swelled, washing across our audience, waxing and waning like the tides. We had worked for two years and had willed ourselves to do the impossible. It was happening. Our last note was magnificent, then gradually diminished to the crystal-clear bell-like tone as when we began, and then difted into the distance.

The curtain closed, and we stood in trance-like silence. Then, without a sound we wrapped our arms around each other and our director. Our tears flowed together as had our music. We had done it!

The curtain reopened. We stood, professionally, awaiting our rating. "Superior rating with commendation. Congratulations!"

We bowed as one body to the thunderous applause. As our heads came up, we were still looking straight ahead into our audience as we had been taught to do. Tears streamed down our faces as we continued to acknowledge the applause.

Salty tears had never tasted so sweet.

TEST TIME

I LOVED SCHOOL EVEN BEFORE I WAS OLD enough to attend. Likewise, I enjoyed almost all of my teachers, including ones who were not so popular. But those ingredients alone didn't make me a straight-A student. I was too busy with extracurricular activities to maintain a 4.0. Also, I was too busy being ornery. Not ornery-ornery, just funny-ornery.

For instance, there was our high school history teacher, Mr. Wigby. He was a conscientious fellow who believed in planning ahead, too far ahead for our own good sometimes. Every day before a history exam, he would stay after-hours in his classroom meticulously filling all three blackboards with his precise, tiny handwriting. He preferred to give us "board" tests rather than typed ones. Later it occurred to me that he might not have been able to type, but, for whatever reason, his tests were recorded on the board and stayed there overnight, patiently waiting for us to take them the next day. He covered them during the day with pull-down maps until test time.

One night several of my friends and I got together at Donita's house to study for a big test the next day. Somewhere during the Civil War discussion, someone in the group wondered out loud whether we would have a certain question on the test.

"I know how we can find out. The test is already on the

171

board. Let's just wander over to school and look for ourselves," challenged Wanda.

The room was suddenly silent as we considered what had just been said. Normally, none of us cheated, but this sounded like fun.

"Oh sure. It's dark. How do we see the board? The test isn't written in braille, you know!"

Everybody laughed as we pictured ourselves blindly running skinny fingers across that blackboard in the dark.

"Yeah, poor old Mr. Wigby would think cockroaches had a party and destroyed his test."

We feverishly made our plans as if we did such things every day. Not one of us ever considered that we might get caught. Anticipation rivaled excitement as we made our way from Donita's house to the high school. Reaching the history room window a few minutes later, our flashlights beamed on Mr. Wigby's tiny, perfectly written sentences. We boldly read them out loud. Our scribe busied herself, calmly taking dictation as several of us tried to give her notes simultaneously.

All six girls and both boys composing the group that night talked and laughed as if this were a normal activity that occurred every day. It was unbelievable.

Suddenly the beam of a flashlight much stronger than any of ours cut through the darkness.

"What are you kids doing?" a heavy male voice boomed from behind. "Trying to break into school?" The voice of authority nailed each of us to the spot where we stood, but paralysis was only momentary. Suddenly all eight of us melted, turning into liquid streaks as someone yelled, "Scatter, it's the cops!"

None of us had ever been in any trouble with the law. In fact, in that little town everybody knew everybody else. The "cops" were men we all knew personally, and they knew us and our parents.

At that moment, with only two policemen and with eight people to be chased, they had to be selective and let some of us kids get away.

"You go after those two, Ben, and I'll get these two girls myself," yelled one policeman to the other.

The two girls he referred to were my friend and I. However, my partner was on the basketball team and could run a lot faster than I could. She had strong leg muscles and made use of them. The only part of me that ran was my fingers! They could race across piano keys when the occasion called for it, but they weren't much help when I was in a footrace for my life.

I could just imagine what my parents would say if the town cop, a good friend of my father's, brought me home. Dad would probably sit down and talk with me, patiently trying to understand just why I had gotten into trouble. Those talks hurt more than all the beatings in the world. At least I thought they did, not being an expert on beatings.

My friend ran as though her feet had suddenly grown wings while I determinedly lumbered in the opposite direction, finding every fresh gopher hole in the high school lawn.

My legs ached as I stepped from one hole into the next, alternately turning one ankle then the other. Moaning, I ran on with Ben gaining on me, easily. I crossed the sidewalk and turned down a side street, but half a block ahead was a streetlight. Ben would be sure to recognize me. Suddenly I left the side street and crossed old Mrs. Langley's back yard. Unfortunately, she was out there.

"What is she doing out here in the dark?" I thought as my sprained ankles were finally putting some distance between me and my pursuer.

"Norene, is that you?" Mrs. Langley screeched.

"No," I puffed. "It's not me—" But my words were cut

short. Quite suddenly I discovered what she had been doing outside in the dark: hanging out her laundry. Having lived there for years, she knew every slope in that yard, and she didn't need a light. But I could have used one about then.

The reason I never finished the sentence was because her low clothesline caught me just under my chin. I must have blacked out for a moment because I don't remember falling. Stumbling to my feet, I charged forward again. Ben was just rounding the corner of her house.

"Norene, dear," Mrs. Langley shouted. "Why are you in such a hurry?"

I could hardly swallow, and my head felt like it was no longer part of my body. However, with visions of Dad's angry blue eyes staring at me, I stumbled on.

Ben stopped to question Mrs. Langley while I maneuvered around to the other side of the house and back toward the street. I could hear them talking.

"Who is it?" Ben demanded.

"It was Norene Murphey. I got a good look at her in the moonlight when she fell. The poor little thing must have cut her throat on my clothesline. She hit it hard enough."

"Oh, that couldn't have been Jeff Murphey's daughter!" Ben assured her. "She would never try to break into the high school. Besides, she's in church every Sunday. No child of Jeff's would do such a thing."

Limping into the shadow of a nearby tree to rest, I promised myself, "I will never do it again!" A full moon had emerged from behind a cloud and bathed the yard in light. You could have heard a pin drop as I stood so still in the shadows until Ben left and Mrs. Langley finally went back into the house.

The next day I wore a scarf at the neck of my dress to hide the heavy bruises on my throat. History was the last period of the day, so by dividing the questions equally eight ways, we soon had all the answers on paper. In a quick conference between classes, we decided to condense the answers by letting Donita type them and give everyone a copy as they came to class.

Word quickly circulated that the history answers would be distributed just before class.

Looking back on events of the previous night got funnier as the day wore on and so had the ever-expanding sequence of events that had occurred. By sixth period everyone in school had heard one or more accounts of "the flashlight adventure."

As sixth period arrived, I stood beside Mr. Wigby in the hall, talking with him and greeting would-be test takers with a small typed strip of paper and a straight pin attached to the top of each one.

"You may need this," I said over and over as I boldly passed out the answers right under Mr. Wigby's nose.

The plan was to pin answers on backs of people seated in front of us and use them as needed. Mr. Wigby would never suspect anything since he always sat at his desk and graded papers while we took our tests. Mr. Wigby wasn't stupid by any means. He was simply unobservant, and never in a million years would he have suspected his honors history class of anything but sterling behavior.

"We aren't really cheating," we had told each other, justifying our actions. It was just a joke! The entire school was in on it by sixth period, and the joke was really on Mr. Wigby. We were so sure we wouldn't get caught; we had made the whole thing a matter of public knowledge.

When the bell rang, everything went as planned. Mr. Wigby went directly to his desk. However, our plan suddenly began to fall apart when one of the boys forgot the answers pinned on his shirt and got up to sharpen a pencil.

"What's pinned to your back, Ray?" asked Mr. Wigby

quietly. I don't think that sweet, mild-mannered little man suspected the truth even then. Trying to be helpful, Mr. Wigby went over to take the paper off Ray's back.

The tension was too much. We all began to giggle, and he laughed right along with us.

"Norene, is this what you were handing out before class?" he innocently inquired.

"Yes, sir," I answered.

The class broke into peals of laughter as one after another related the events of our flashlight adventure. Mr. Wigby's eyes widened, then he laughed along with us. Finally, wiping away his tears, that good-natured old man turned to me.

"What are you planning to do, my dear Norene, if you live to grow up?"

"I'm going to be a teacher," I told him. This time the class rolled in laughter.

That observation was a prophecy. Loving practical jokes has kept me ahead of my students for years—but sometimes only by a step or two.

THE ORAL BOOK REPORT

I ALWAYS LOVED TO TELL STORIES, TRUE ones or otherwise. Because of my love for language, spoken and written, the oral book report was my favorite English assignment.

While most of my classmates suffered insomnia or dreamed a string of embarrassing nightmares, I read book after book, searching for one with just the right amounts of drama and humor. Finally discovered, I practiced verbalizing the scary sections and putting the finishing touches on the humor. I waited in eager anticipation for "my turn" and stretched that cherished time as long as I could. Not until I reached the eighth grade did I meet a teacher who was willing to indulge my verboseness to its absolute limits.

Miss Mary Jo Rodrick was a favorite of everybody. She loved kids. She loved teaching, and she smiled all the time. We blossomed in the glow of her love, and oh how we produced.

It was in her class that I first dared take more than one entire period—an hour in length—for my favorite of all assignments, the oral book report. For me it was as natural as breathing. Delighting as she did in whatever her students produced, she was the best audience I'd ever had. She clapped, she laughed out loud, she screamed in the scary parts, and she fed my starving ego, adding fuel to my verbal fire.

The book was a mystery, and everyone was on the edge of their seats. The wind howled, the sea roared, and ghosts screamed as they pushed the creaking mansion off the bluff onto the rocks below. By the end of the first period, I was only a few pages into the novel. It would continue into the next day. The following day was more of the same. We crept down dark, shadowy underground passageways feeling spider webs on our faces as rats scurried about our feet. We were pursued by bats and evil spirits, and a madman chased us through a cemetery. Day two ended as day one had, and still the story hung in midair.

The third day was more of the same, and students from other rooms asked about the story. Day four was followed by more chills than all the others put together. At the end of day four, Miss Rodrick announced that I would finish on Friday.

I'd never had so much fun in my life. Watching my classmates cringing, screaming, and scooting down into their chairs, I was in my element. I had found my addiction: storytelling, acting, creating an atmosphere of whatever I imagined.

On the fifth and final day I baptized my audience in the finale. We lived it together. The story had never lived before, and we experienced it now—together—fresh as it unfolded there in front of us.

For the remainder of the year, I was allowed a week for my oral book report. Few, if any, other teachers would have been so tolerant, but, looking back, I believe she sincerely enjoyed those performances almost as much as I did.

Was that time wasted on one student? I would like to think it wasn't because it was a precious time for me. That year I began giving oral book reviews for women's clubs and civic groups. I had numerous offers from the clubs in town, and the people were always gracious and encouraging. We lived through many stories together, and they appeared to love it as much as I.

I was never confused. After that, I knew what I wanted to do. I wanted to teach, to go into the classroom and create that magic atmosphere where people would learn and love learning. A fine teacher is an actor, a storyteller, a creator of magic who swings open doors of the mind that may have been locked or undiscovered. She has to be able to accept the fact that not all students will buy that magic; some of them won't even like it. But they will know they have been in the presence of something special. They may not be ready, or they may be too far removed emotionally and mentally to participate. But the fairy dust will have touched them, and it will remain an unforgettable experience.

In the glow of Miss Mary Jo Rodrick's confident smile and the presence of her encouraging heart, the door of my future swung wide open. The subject of my love would be introduced a little later, but the lights came up on my world in my eighth-grade year during the oral book report.

COMMUNICATION

MARY JO RODRICK INTRODUCED ME TO Lucile Waller, the high school principal. Sometimes director of the yearbook, when not in charge of the school-newspaper, she was director of the annual and the teacher of speech and drama classes.

We struck an instant friendship. This tiny woman had enough energy to move the whole school, and she did. She loved people, and it showed as she met even her fiercest opponents, if she really had any, with a smile. She had so much confidence in her students it was almost easy to do whatever she asked. She knew her students could do anything, and they did.

I was in her speech class my first year in high school. She created an atmosphere that made learning possible, then she stepped back and let us create the language that painted the pictures. We read, we argued, we verbalized, and we read some more. We presented plays, painted sets, hunted props, and gave productions. None of these plays had famous names, but the experiences served their purpose.

Speech tournaments followed, and we participated confidently. Sure we were scared, but not much. We were "Lucile's Kids," and she somehow always had the good ones. We competed, and we won, at least most of the time. But trophies weren't everything. Learning was, and we learned.

One time I had entered both humorous and dramatic literature interpretation, but I hated the humorous selection. The dramatic piece allowed me the privilege, I felt, to empty all my dramatic barrels. I could cry real tears, and I did. I usually took the audience with me. I loved it!

Lucile encouraged me to enter and prepare the humorous piece, but I wouldn't listen. Finally she made me a deal: Read it for Mother and Dad, and if they didn't like it, I could forget about it. I read it, and they both cried from laughing so hard. A deal was a deal, but the tournament was the next day. There wasn't time for memorization.

I remember Daddy telling me to just memorize the general sequence of events and give the dialogue impromptu. That was risky, if not suicidal, but it was the only choice left.

At the competition, I thought the drama round was excellent. I cried tons of tears, both judges cried, and one finally left the room completely overcome, I thought. That had to mean success.

In humorous lit I winged it. Lucile sat in the back attempting to follow the book if I got lost. I got lost from the book all right—one glance at her told me it might not be in the book at all. She was frantically turning pages without success. But the story flowed. I did the "oral book report routine," although the sequence was wrong. The audience enjoyed it, and so did I, but Lucile was in a state of shock.

"Where did you get some of that stuff?" she laughed later. "It was new to me."

"Yeah, it was to me, too—when stuck, make it up—and I did!"

"Well, it worked. So don't worry about it."

I performed it twice more that day, and each time it was different.

"Oh, well, it's Russian roulette anyway." My dramatic tears would rival the Barrymores'. "That's the one I live for," I crowed.

But at the end of the competition, the humorous impromptu "book report" won first place, and the tons of tears got lost somewhere.

"Maybe you'd better never memorize anything again," Lucile laughed on the way home. "If you can 'oral book report' your way to first place, why not?"

But I wasn't that confident. Lucky, maybe. There was something unprofessional about making up a story "kinda like that one." So next time I did my homework.

During those years with Miss Waller, I discovered the subject I'd teach and love and share for a lifetime: communication. So many people find it intimidating to face an audience and attempt to make sense of what they have to say. Helping them do that is my gift, and I've loved every minute of it through the years.

Creating the magic atmosphere of love and respect within the classroom is step one, but furnishing people with faith to try out their words in front of a friendly audience has been the thrill of my lifetime. To help them believe in their ability to create magic through their own unique personalities has been the final step for me.

On the first day of a beginning communications class, the faces looking back are full of pure fear: fear of failure, fear of embarrassment, fear of discovering they really are stupid.

I tell them on the first day that this is the class they will always remember and may very well enjoy the most. That brings frowns and groans. But I tell them when class is finished, they won't want it to be over. That brings cynical laughter. But I have found through the years that on the last day of classes, that is almost always the case. Goodbyes are hard to say when so much has been shared.

Lucile Waller was one of my mentors, the most important one. She was the one who turned on the lights of the runway to my future.

I have met the grandest people in my communication classes. Many of my dearest and longest friendships began there. It has been a precious time and a place where the magic broke through. We each experienced the beauty of the individual, not only as we are, but as we would like to be.

Our dreams, hopes, fears, and our faith have bound us together in love as we learned to give words to those things and in the expression, to give ourselves away to each other. That is the magic we call communication.

SPECIAL MENTORS

SOUTHERN CALIFORNIA WAS FINALLY experiencing an end to another drought of several years. Rain poured down as heavy, but welcome, rain clouds darkened midday into night. The deluge was closing freeways and making life generally miserable at Pasadena City College.

This year, as in numerous past ones, the spring speech championship was in full swing. Colleges and universities from all over southern California, and a few from neighboring states, had sent their students to compete. Gathered in the crowded judges' lounge, a misnomer for an uncomfortable classroom, coaches from all of the represented schools stood around the buffet table. Ballots weren't out yet for the next round, and Tony, the highly respected older coach and television professor at Pasadena, was serving up a round of his personal goodies. Such service was not the norm, but when Tony did something, he did it well. That not only included his classes in radio and television but the movies he wrote, directed, and produced for ABC with the help of his students.

The moment was poignant. Tony was a mentor to many of us in the room, an encourager and adviser. In some ways he was rather like a grandfather figure: a dear and valued friend.

Looking back, I realized I had known many people who had similar influence, not necessarily because of their professional standing but because they had cared when I really needed it. It was once called "heart."

I had grown up with a whole cadre of would-be grand-parents, those elderly men and women on Main Street who had adopted me. Most of them were widows or widowers, and they had few, if any, children living there in town.

From the time I started competing in speech tourna-ments, my own private cheering section often gathered at Dad's café and drank coffee until I returned from a tour-nament with the wild tales of the day. I never failed to win something because there seemed to be an obligation to these dear people. They expected good things to hap-pen, and they did. These elderly people had little to look forward to except the small excitements, such as they were, on Main Street. So that little crew became my "many adopted grandpas." A few of the elderly ladies fit into that extended family, but they rarely went anywhere at night.

On holidays like Thanksgiving, Christmas, and Easter, Mother and Daddy closed the café to regular business. White tablecloths were starched stiff and the tables deco-rated simply for the occasion. Then all of those people who had nowhere else to go came and ate the holiday dinner as part of our family. It was a special time for all of us.

I remember one tournament in high school when the competition was especially difficult. For three years one talented, attractive young woman had been my fiercest competitor. That last year at state, we were pitted against each other again. She was self-confident and almost cocky in her determination.

As we renewed our friendship, she casually said, "You know, I'm going to win this year. Daddy is buying me a new convertible if I do. I'll be sixteen next week."

I looked at her and quietly said, "That isn't a good enough reason."

"Oh, what better one is there?"

I explained matter-of-factly that I had all of these adopted grandparents at home and that I just couldn't afford to let them down.

"That's the dumbest reason I ever heard," she responded honestly. And to her it might have been dumb. For me, though, it was the extra push I needed to get me across the finish line. The hugs and slaps on the back and the "that's the way to go, honey" meant more to me than all of the bribes in the world.

As I look back now, there have been several Tonys: great teachers, mentors like Dr. Dina Stallings and Opal Cole Craig, and Dr. Barbara McIntyre. But all of them weren't teachers—including my elderly cheering section—and all of them didn't have Ph.D.s. They didn't need them.

GRADUATION

"**W**AS LAST NIGHT WILD OR WHAT?"

"Last night was crazy," I agreed. "I still can't believe what happened to our baccalaureate service."

"Me either! Norene, when you finished singing, it sounded like the music shifted into overdrive. I mean, with that tornado warning connecting to the last note of your song like that, it was just wild!"

The entire graduating class was laughing by now.

"I almost took off with it," I replied, recalling the previous night. "The tornado alarm was in another key, but it got my attention and quick!"

"You should have seen your face. You looked too angelic while you were singing, but when that alarm went off your expression sure changed. I thought you were going to jump into the orchestra pit with the band!"

"Me, too! I was looking for a place to hide in a hurry!"

Our senior class was robed and waiting to march down the aisle at the high school auditorium for the last time. Tonight was graduation.

The previous night we had solemnly marched down front, taken our seats, and begun the religious service that preceded graduation. The school auditorium was full all the way to the back. Each year the churches in town dismissed their evening services on the Sunday night before graduation. The pastors of each of the churches were responsible for the various parts of the baccalaureate program, and the privilege of "bringing the message" was rotated so that eventually each denomination was represented. The previous night's service, however, had been different from any anyone could remember.

After our serious, slow march down the aisle and the quiet prayer that followed, I had begun to sing "The End of a Perfect Day." Just as my last word ended, we were jarred back to reality by the low groan of the fire alarm. However, when it hung on its highest note for what seemed a full minute, we knew more than the volunteer firemen would be leaving. It signaled a tornado sighting. For a moment we all stared at each other. Then the superintendent stepped to the speaker's stand.

"As quickly and orderly as possible, please leave the building. Seek immediate shelter. We are dismissed. Have a safe trip home."

The storm hadn't been a complete surprise. The clouds had been building all afternoon. Even as we entered the school building, lightning flashed furiously in the southwest and thunder grumbled close by. But this was our baccalaureate service, we had reasoned, and no one of us would have missed it.

The outcome was anticlimactic. The wind had blown and it had rained, but the storm had been short-lived. Now tonight would be our last official night together.

"Pomp and Circumstance" played by the high school band began its usual slow, sad dirge. We claimed our alphabetical places in line and faced the auditorium door.

"This is it, you guys! It's all over but the celebrating," yelled someone in the rear. "After this it's the senior trip, and we are out of here!"

Some class members yelled in happy response, but many of us didn't. I didn't want it all to be over. I was growing up now, accepting responsibility for facing the world. It was scary. I had loved being little, loved growing up, loved these people in my class. I loved this little town. I loved Main Street and all of the good times—and even the bad times—I had here.

As we processed slowly to our seats, parents, grandparents, and a townful of friends turned toward us. This was the moment of triumph we had worked twelve years to achieve. We knew everyone in the audience of well-wishers.

Knowing and being known hadn't always been this great. In a town this small it often felt like people knew more about our business—my business—than I did, and I had resented that at times. But usually I enjoyed it. These people were family, and we had been through a lot together.

In a few minutes we would hold our high school diplomas in our hands. There would be applause and gifts, then we would go our ways.

Several people in our class were getting married. A few already had. A few had jobs, but most of the jobs were away from here. Several of us were going away to college. So this was "good byo."

Good-bye to Main Street. Good-bye to test taking and ball games. Good-bye to meeting friends at the corner drugstore after school. Good-bye to growing up and the good times.

Main Street had nourished each of us in its own way, helping us to develop our own uniqueness. Here, where people had time to encourage and—yes—criticize us and know us individually, we had grown up. We were ready to meet the world because of the strength we had developed and the love we had been given.

In a sense, most of us already had outgrown this place we had called home. Most of us would leave, never to return. America was growing up, and we were growing with it.

Graduation was just the official good-bye. Our triumph tonight was bittersweet because of it.

I'M NEVER GOING BACK!

LIKE MANY OF US WHO ORIGINATED IN small-town America, I promised myself when I left, "I'm never going back!" There was nothing to do, and nothing to look forward to professionally. I have almost been true to that promise.

Actually, as the years go by, I'm becoming more loyal than I ever intended. The lights on Main Street have become candles lighting the lanes of my childhood memories, those incidents that shaped my life and made me who I am.

Like long shadows stretching down the street, the values I learned there made permanent imprints on my mind. I have returned spiritually thousands of times. I learned that one person can make a difference; to see people as individuals, not faceless crowds; to respect others, which in turn brought respect. I learned about concern for others and love for my fellow man.

Yes, I had learned discrimination. Lines drawn in the sand can become impenetrable walls, whether of race, religion, or society.

But most of all I had learned that taking time to love changes our world, that taking time to listen shows the measurement of care, that a group of people working together can make life's struggles and sorrows bearable.

All these basic values had their geneses on Main Street.

Although I vowed I would never go home again, my heart has returned again and again, and each time it draws strength for another tomorrow.